RISE TO THE SUN

*Dear Edna Lee and Jim,*

# RISE TO THE SUN

## 7 Footsteps and 7 Prayers
## for Getting Out of Hell

*My warmest good wishes,*
*With love,*
*Richard*

### Richard J. Marks

*May 2020*
*New York City*

NEW DEGREE PRESS

COPYRIGHT © 2020 RICHARD J. MARKS

RISE TO THE SUN

*7 Footsteps and 7 Prayers for Getting Out of Hell*

Cover design by Gjorgji Pejkovski
Interior design by Zoran Maksimović

ISBN

978-1-64137-562-7   *Paperback*
978-1-64137-563-4   *Kindle Ebook*
978-1-64137-564-1   *Digital Ebook*

# Contents

---

# PART 2

The progression of the seven footsteps and seven prayers asserts a format of change: from hopelessness, trauma and grief, to being worthy of love; and as we find it within, we begin sharing the inner journey of freedom with others.

## Breaking Free

PRAYER
### "Breaking Free from Sorrow"
By Richard J. Marks

## Don't Believe the Pain

PRAYER
from *In The Shelter*
By Pádraig Ó Tuama

## The Big Goodbye

PRAYER
from *The Glass Bead Game*
By Hermann Hesse

## Personal Responsibility - Relationships

PRAYER
### "Daily Moral Inventory"
By an anonymous committee

# PART 3

We travel our freedom differently in West and East, North and South, but ultimately, how we travel inwardly is the same as how we travel outwardly.

## Epilogue: Freedom Travels

PRAYER
## "Creed for Awakening"
By Richard J. Marks

## About the Book

## Bibliography

# Acknowledgments

**To the readers of this book**, for taking a leap away from the things that tie us down and for moving in the direction of personal and community transformation, may we gather with greater stability and strength in every conceivable way.

**The making of this book** was built on the love, entrepreneurial creativity and limitless confidence of Eric Koester, Founder, Creator Institute and Professor of Practice, Georgetown University's McDonough School of Business; this book's healing purpose was developed and strengthened by the subtle and lyrical hands of Whitney Elaine Jones, Editor, Creator Institute; the central anchor and mainstay to all new creative authors, Brian Bies, Head of Publishing, New Degree Press; the magic guidance of Kristy Carter, Editor, New Degree Press; and everyone at New Degree Press who are hard at work hatching writers and original books.

**With gratitude to Tom Weirich**, an unwavering brother and fellow journeyman, this book began almost overnight when he brought me and the Creator Institute together, sheltered me, believed in me, and never once told me to be quiet as I strove to find voice for the stories in the book that essentially say: our hearts are ready for a change. We have been dutiful and done work to be proud of, but it's what inside that counts; may we now walk lighter and in freedom.

**For the brave women and men interviewed in this book,** each of whom have struggled with pain and grief and come through to the other side, you replaced the mantle of the teachers of the past and are now our living teachers.

**From my charming and versatile mother Yonah Louise Marks,** a beautiful Romantic artist and beloved Friend in this lifetime whose ancient Hebrew name Yonah יוֹנָה means "dove" and who has endured dissatisfaction, sorrow, and loss but shown no weakness in pursuit of adventure, I have learned that "when you stop managing everything, miracles happen — the logs that you placed in your way get lifted, and it's very pleasant."

**Honoring our ancestors,** we do not need to apologize for our damage but to be worthy ancestors ourselves.

**The people interviewed for this book,** whose love is at the core of every battle, I revere your courage:

| | |
|---|---|
| Nancy B. Black | JoAnn Wright Milliken |
| Tamara Buchwald | Jessica Rockwood |
| Kathy Eldon | Marc-Olivier Strauss-Kahn |
| Tim McHenry | The Rev. Eva Suarez |
| Winsome McIntosh | Tom Vendetti |

# With Gratitude:

Susan Agostinelli & Dave Michalski
Patricia Altshuler
Helen Gomez Andrews
Margarite Arsinoë
John Arundel
Jim Allison
Corinne Arnold
Alexandra H. Ballard
Janelle Balnicke
Grace Beacham
Lincoln Benet
Eric Berman
Kate Warrick-Berman & Jeff Berman
Joan & Phil Berman
Mary Berman
Sarah Berman
Lisa Bittan
Susan Blackmoor
Christopher Boutlier
Gerlinde Brixius
Tamara Buchwald
Colin Bridge
Amy & Terry Britton
Misia Broadhead & Anthony Barham
Sabina Broadhead & Francis Freisinger
Patricia & Dario Campanile
Elizabeth Cargo
The Carlyle Hotel, New York City
Kevin Chaffee
William Bryan Cheek

Gregory Cohen

Julia Cohen & Neil Barrett

Gertrude Zinner d'Amecourt *(in sweet remembrance)*

Marion & Guy d'Amecourt

Nicole d'Amecourt

Melton Kalehua Darneal

Loren Davis

Alexandra Dwek

Alexandra & Joe Dwek

Jonathan Dwek

Carole L. Feld

Daniel Foa

The Rev. Ryan Fleenor

Izette Folger

Megan Gabriel

Saundra Gibson

Sharon Girard

Kim Goodman

Cynthia Guyer

Tyrone Hall

Nora, Todd & William Hathaway

Lisa Nicole Henson

Bill Hillendahl

Wendolyn Holland

Berna Huebner

The Rev. Brenda Husson

Fabian Huwyler

Brandy Hyman

Yves Kamioner

Lisa Marks Phillips Karr

Scodina Kenny

Quinn, Parker & Aven Koester

Sara Lake

Elizabeth Levings

Anne Levonen

David C. Levy

Rob Long

Lily Berman Lopez & Adam Lopez

Ann K. Luskey

Michael Maccoby

Sandylee Maccoby *(in sweet remembrance)*

Sarah A. Malachowsky

Helen Marks, Gabriel Legendy & Westley Marks Legendy

Jane London Marks

Hon. Marc Lincoln Marks *(in sweet remembrance)*

JoAnn Mason

Janet McCartney

Renee B. Miller

Alison Mize

David Nieves

Elizabeth M. Parella

Gail Percy

Lake Perriguey

Andrea Pollan

Prince Harry, Duke of Sussex

Jill Ragsdale

Adam Ratajczak

Holly Ritchie

Timothy Rockwood

Dana Rooney

Margery Arent Safir

St. James' Church, New York City

Nick Sanchez

Priya & Michael Sanger

Nick Sangermano

Ariun Sanjaajamts

Patrick Sasso

Liesl Schillinger

Rob Schwartz

Mark Sheehan

Deborah Sigmund

Julia Simmons

Chéri Faso Olf

Lindsey & Mike Smith

Philip Grady Smith

Satisha Smith

Rowan Soeiro

Sancho Soeiro

Dwight L. Stuart, Jr.

The Rev. Zachary Thompson

George D. Vassiliou

Cecilia "Sam" Vessel

Edna Lee Warnecke & Jim Marks

Jean Weille

Tom Weirich

Gregory Wendt

Christine Harper Whitaker

Vince Wilcke

Xiaogang Zhang

Richard J. Marks, *Incandescence at Sunset,*
La Teste-de-Buch, 2015.

Situated in the middle of La forêt des
Landes (Landes forest) and south
of Bassin d'Arcachon (Arcachon Bay) in
southwestern France.

"*My destination is no longer a
place, but a new way of seeing.*"

-Marcel Proust,
French novelist (1871-1922)

# Dedication

———

Nearly seventy-five years have passed since the famed and eclectic British novelist of *Brave New World* (1932), Aldous Huxley, wrote autobiographically in *The Art of Seeing* (1942). His lifelong eyesight problems that started when he was a schoolboy had become so pronounced that the tragedy of complete blindness was fast approaching.

In pursuit of help, Huxley turned to an unheard-of method by American ophthalmologist, Dr. William Bates (1860-1931), who claimed relaxation is key to vision improvement. Dr. Bates' book entitled *The Bates Method for Better Eyesight Without Glasses*, first published as *Perfect Sight Without Glasses* in 1920, went so far that he disagreed with the generally accepted Helmholtz theory of vision, which in fact has prevailed until today.

The most famous eye specialist in Britain fiercely denounced Huxley's exuberance as well as Bates' unheard-of method as quackery: not scientific, utterly unorthodox, unconventional, and untested. Untested or not, Huxley faced an advancing and inevitable blindness that would have curtailed his life's work, his ability to read and write, so the notion that he could put off or even avoid such a future ignited him. He accepted the theory that artificial lenses (eyeglasses) were making his eyes weaker.

Huxley took personal responsibility for something immensely hopeful. He learned why he needed to strengthen his own weakened and atrophied eye muscles. The methods employed were actual physical exercises for relaxing and healing of the muscles of his eyes, which worked well for him. Blindness receded, and he cultivated a keen ability to see life outwardly. Despite all, he emerged afresh with the ability to see the world 1) without eyeglasses, 2) no longer as a fixed point to be stared at (myopia), and 3) as a constantly widening field. In other words, he gained the ability to see the world expansively, beyond a routine old-world-order.

Simply put, it was a total re-training, from muscle to mind.

The retraining of mind and body Huxley experienced is relevant in the twenty-first century. At the beginning of this new decade, we can imagine seeing the world with wonder once again simply by taking personal responsibility for the water we drink, the land we farm, and the air we breathe. We all touch the code of life—and to bring fresh awareness into our bodies, we must be sincere in the challenge of being brave enough to bring a higher standard to bear.

I've traveled deep into some of the least populated ancient cultural frontiers—China's Gobi Desert, Mongolia's vast grasslands, Greenland's icecaps, America's oldest forests, Hawaii's interplay of positive ionic and volcanic—finding intimacy with Nature and fresh connection with spiritual traditions.

This book's purpose is inspired by the "Chant of Metta." The Pali word 'metta' means loving-kindness, friendliness, good-will, benevolence, fellowship, amity, concord, and non-violence; it has been described as a 'pure font of well-being and safety for others.' The Hawaiian concept of 'Pono'—doing the right thing—is a potent added ingredient with the dimension of hope, equity, and goodness.

The crux of self-discovery demands knowing what to do with freedom and how to participate in it. This book teaches and guides us to see with fresh eyes, by retraining ourselves, so we can restore freedom to our lives.

Ida Ten Eyck O'Keeffe (1889-1961). *Variation on a Lighthouse Theme IV*, 1931-1932. Oil on canvas.

Image courtesy Dallas Museum of Art,
photo: Brad Flowers. Jeri L. Wolfson Collection.

This rendition of Cape Cod's Highland Lighthouse by Ida O'Keeffe, an artist every bit as gifted and lustrous as her older sister Georgia O'Keeffe, continues to represent strength, guidance, and hope. When feeling like voyagers at sea and scared of the unknown, in the midst of the darkness, a glimmer of light will emerge. It's our choice to follow it.

# Prologue

---

Many people believe that to 'fix' ourselves and the world, we need to 'do' things differently. I believe something else: we need to see things differently.

This book delves into transforming ourselves before we can transform the world. The seven footsteps and seven prayers assert a format for change: we are ready to reprogram ourselves, rather than be programmed by outside forces.

Before tackling change in the world, remember activism is being reactive: when something bad happens, we feel we need to 'do something about it.' It may even be altruistic, such as when people freely open their homes on Airbnb, at no charge, to people and animals escaping their homes during California's extreme fires or Florida's increasing hurricanes.

But even such acts of decency don't change what is happening: we are running.

Nowadays, the absence of courtesy and basic respect also reflects our inner crisis. Even young people are speaking up and asking: what point is there in following an education in a world that has no future?

A red-alert button gets pressed: 'do something!' We feel a need to respond to the message that 'to do nothing is the craziest thing we can do.' Catastrophes are happening right before our eyes on a scale we can't even imagine. We are distracted by what is threatening. The potential dangers compel us to remain ever-ready to react.

In the course of my life, 'healing the heart' has been calling to me. Because I didn't yet understand how to heal my own, I became good at helping other people, and as an environmentalist, I have worked to heal the earth.

My first week at work in Washington DC during the Recovery Act of 2009, I met a career program manager in geological and earth sciences packing his boxes on his way to retirement. As an energy communications specialist in the Office of Energy Efficiency and Renewable Energy at the US Department of Energy, I was optimistic to be here—to promote widespread renewable energy finally on the rise. Why, then, was his mood dark and stifled?

He invited me into his office to see, before pulling them down, a horizontal stretch of time-faded photographs on the wall. "See that? And that? And that?" Each one the ghost of an installed clean energy power plant built across America. We want to believe the world is beginning to shift from the Industrialization Age to Post-Carbon Age; breakthrough innovations are desperately needed to find solutions in a fresh framework to engage and usher more people into a better world. But his declaring, not sourly as much as sadly that "nothing ever got done," instantly deflated my optimism with a sharp question: *"Why should things be any different now?"*

In anything that people feel they need to fight for or against, anger can be a very creative stimulus, but indignities that go on for too long can stick so hard that they calcify. What good is marching if you feel it's come today, gone tomorrow? What good is running for public office if you can't sustain a way to uplift people? Why save the environment if you are feeling worthless inside? Why bother changing jobs or cities or relationships if you keep finding disappointments?

Readers of this book may feel stuck, as in Paul's lament "For I have the desire to do what is good, but I cannot carry it out," which essentially points out that we do the things we don't want to do and don't do the things we want to do. For those of us who don't want to feel forever stuck in hell—which is our own innate freedom corrupted—it's time to come forth for the sake of our own heart and soul. As we begin the progression for seeing things differently, remember the body and mind may have become addicted to negativity or to 'fixing' everything, but the soul is not addicted.

Pauses are important; silence is of the essence sometimes. Each turning to a new page is intended to allow the reader to reflect, if she or he wants to do so.

Every chapter of this book includes prayers, which are not exclusively religious. Prayers are the ultimate expressions of human feeling. Prayer is a way of shifting more easily, from moment to moment, to something greater than oneself. Prayer is feeling and seeing beauty in the world. Singing songs and hearing music, rather than reading words from books.

*The New York Times* foreign correspondent C. L. Sulzberger was a well-known atheist who collected a lifetime's worth of prayers, from all times past. He came to the beautiful insight that prayer is 'human truth.'

> The Pew Research Center's 2014 Religion and Public Life study, *Frequency of Prayer* (sample size = 35,071), puts the percentage of adults who pray daily at fifty-five percent. It breaks down by religious groups, age, gender, racial and ethnic composition, immigrant status, income, education, marital status, belief in God, and frequency of participation in scripture study or meditation.
>
> Most interestingly, the percentage of all adults who feel a sense of spiritual peace and well-being from praying at least daily is very high: 76 percent; weekly 49 percent; monthly 34 percent; and seldom/never 30 percent.
>
> I am one of the 76 percent of people who has found well-being, but first, I needed to see that prayer is not what I thought it was.

Using prayer, active at every step of the way, allows us to gain the awareness we seek to keep pressing forward, perhaps not knowing the outcomes but realizing we have hope where there was little or none before. We all have access to it.

Importantly, you will see consistently that the journey of this book, every step of the way, is about building good relationships.

Healing starts with self-love: that natural impulse and awareness where we finally stop causing ourselves harm. That can be anything: old traumas; serving two or more masters; hiding our light, our self, our love; forgetting who loves us or forgetting that you love yourself; running in fear; refusing a communal life, preventing intimacy, going mute or cold. As the philosopher and psychologist Erich Fromm (1900-1980) proposed, "Loving oneself means caring about oneself, respecting oneself, and knowing oneself."

Making myself better is my story of survival and expansion. Personal responsibility is about learning how to knit together these two transformations: inner (our own soul) and external (making the world better).

Over the past five years, I've been on a journey to find out how all of us can stop trying to *do* things differently and start to *see* things differently. The results have reframed the way I see the world.

We can begin repairing our response to trauma and the grief that we carry inside ourselves. But as much as the work of healing ourselves is important, we must not stay in that space.

The goal of renewing and transforming ourselves is to feel better about serving others and planetary issues.

A friend called me from a brief trip to Sri Lanka—a trip so brief that his only outing was to be shown around a spectacular gem of a nineteenth-century Buddhist temple in Colombo.

It is the Gangaramaya Temple, which follows the steps of the Buddha himself: it is involved in welfare work, constructing old peoples' homes, a vocational school, and an orphanage.

He called to ask whether I knew, when I gave this book its title, that in Buddhism, seven is the number of ascent, and Buddha is said to have walked this number of footsteps at his birth.

I'm not a Buddhist but to quote Buddha: "Drop by drop is the water pot filled. Likewise, the wise man, gathering it little by little, fills himself with good." Spiritual healing is a drop-by-drop process in which we fill ourselves with good. And, though the word 'spiritual' can scare people off, it is a part of us, grounded in our core as human beings, and cutting across any sort of religious divide. Every footstep is a progression—a way of life unfolding toward the 'heart of the matter.'

My personal journey of 'getting out of hell' speaks to spiritual healing. For four decades, I felt as if I were on an eternal safari, from China to Canada, Los Angeles to Washington DC, San Francisco to New York City, Santa Fe to Boulder.

The story of my quest is for anyone who wants to get out of hell and get 'unstuck' from pain, whether caused by the past, or the tumultuous and impossible twenty-first-century present. I write about it to chart and illuminate the passage to the other side of grief and hopelessness, whether it is inside our heart or about the world at large. My hope is that you also will discover and desire, more than ever, to break free, retrain yourself, and find freedom.

Each of the following chapters corresponds to a 'footstep' as a way of life and action.

In step one, we *'break free.'* We see how helping others (even when we are most down) makes us stronger. We pull up the weeds, all those disappointments and difficulties that make us feel we can't do anything no matter what we try to do.

In step two, we *'don't believe the pain.'* We let our sincerity and surrender be genuine and complete, helping us reject selfishness and the trappings of the mind.

In step three, we open our entire beings to *'seeing hope'* where there was hopelessness. Forms of energy healing arise. The truth of energy healing is that we are energetic and, therefore, can be healed. We begin to restore physical health.

We encounter a turning point toward freedom and away from living in hell. We say, *'The Big Goodbye.'* Once we are aware there is no higher value than freedom of living and freedom of expression, we cross a threshold. We start to see we can become unshaken and that we shall pass through the ordeal.

In step four, we see it is time to *'take personal responsibility for relationships.'* Societies create a world in which it's easy for us to be isolated. We have to see that it's just as easy not to be isolated and how we can create relationships that move us out of hell.

In step five, a *'three-way-path to seeing'* begins: Break Free; Retrain Yourself; Find Freedom.

We understand how **'being worthy of love'** can prevail in a society where people are closed off and alienated from each other. What is required is an inner change; freedom does not come from outer circumstances but from inner liberation. We have **'freedom to share'** and know we are worthy of love.

In step six, we **'make friends'**—the Earth becomes our friend again as we see ourselves becoming mindful of our relationship with all living things.

In step seven, instead of coming to the end, we come to a **'new beginning'** when we ask: **'what is this thing called Love?'**

Yet, to get prepared for this journey to freedom and its seven footsteps, we need first to **'flush the psychic toilet'** and, second, to realize that **'prayer is for everyone'** is a way of seeing human truth. Along each of the seven footsteps we take together on this journey, you'll find prayers to open the eyes and the heart.

Let's start now.

One prayer that rises above the rest for me is 'I pray for myself one thing above all: expansion of my heart's freedom.'

Richard J. Marks. *Les Trois Tetons* (The Three Breasts), 2014.
At the 4,000-meter Grand Teton peak, Grand Teton National Park in the northwest of the US state of Wyoming, linked to nearby Yellowstone National Park.

*"Honesty is very hard. The truth is often painful. But the freedom it can bring is worth the trying."*

- Fred Rogers (1928-2003),
American television personality, writer, puppeteer, and Presbyterian minister who wrote and produced 912 episodes of *Mr. Rogers' Neighborhood* from 1968 to 2001.

# Flushing the Psychic Toilet

––––

## Mae West and Me: The End of Freedom

At the age of seven, I was already carrying enough pain and despair that I devised plans to kill myself by running the car in a closed garage. I can remember a whole week of walking myself through the steps like a rehearsal. At fifteen, I nearly succeeded. When, in 1984, my mother awoke at 3:45 a.m. one morning to have a stern talk with me, I was almost not breathing from the 500 pills I had taken with some wine. The paramedic who took me to the University of California San Francisco Medical Center told her, "God sent you to his room today."

One sunny day in 1978, we drove across the flat horizon of Los Angeles and entered a time vortex. My mother and her husband, a recipient of the Purple Heart for his service in Normandy and the events of the D-Day invasion, turned the car into the driveway of an old-Hollywood-era estate that would become my home for the next three years.

The all-white American Colonial-style buildings, with their turned paneled woods and beige Spanish tiled roofs, sat immaculately nestled throughout the manicured estate's old gardens and giant Queen Palms. No evidence here betrays that Mae West—described by Molly Haskell as the "the blond, diamond-studded, wisecracking, sashaying vamp from Brooklyn who lit up the stage in the 1920s and the screen in the 1930s with a special brand of gender-bending sexuality"—ever slept here, let alone owned it.

*Parade Formation*, Ridgewood Military Academy, Woodland Hills, California.

## Mae West. Talk about freedom.

The bawdy Mae West films were uncensored until a national campaign in 1934, which battled "film immorality," forced her to follow the rules of the Production Code Administration (PCA), which is the film industry's self-regulatory organization. Was it the words in her 1933 films *She Done Him Wrong* and *I'm No Angel* that led to censorship or was it the fact that a woman was saying them, a woman who made bad seem good and refused to honor the dichotomy between virgin and whore?

"When I'm good I'm good... but when I'm bad, I'm better."

"It's not the men in your life... it's the life in your men."

Suitor: "If only I could trust you."

West: "You can... hundreds have."

In 1978, I am ten and Mae West is eighty-five.

My mother, her husband, and I step out of the car, into an America running on multiple realities.


## One reality in 1978.
Mae West has returned to the screen in *Sextette*. When asked, "Do you get a lot of proposals from your male fans?" she quips, "Yeah, and what they propose is nobody's business." *The New York Times* called *Sextette* "embarrassing," and said, "Granny should have her mouth washed out with soap, along with her teeth."

"Too much of a good thing can be wonderful," jested Hollywood sex symbol of the
1930s and master of the double entendre, Mae West (1892-1980), photographed by
English society photographer Allan Warren in her sitting room in Hollywood.

## Another reality.

Harvey Milk, the first openly gay person to be elected to public office in California, will be assassinated on November 27, 1978.

*San Francisco Examiner* headline, Nov. 27, 1978.

## Another?

The anti-military sentiments of the Vietnam War, which ended officially in 1975, continue to overturn the country's wartime value systems. John F. Kerry saw "Courage both in the Vietnam War and in the struggle to stop it." He learned that "patriotism includes protest, not just military service."

John Kerry, twenty-seven, testified about the war in Vietnam before the Senate Foreign Relations Committee on April 22, 1971, long before he was elected a United States senator.

## Another?

The highest-rated show on television from 1971 to 1976 and one of the greatest shows and TV writing of all time—*All in the Family*—gives voice to America's pervasive racism, homophobia, and women's liberation.

*All In the Family* cast Carroll O'Connor (Archie Bunker), Jean Stapleton (Edith Bunker), Sally Struthers (Gloria Bunker Stivic) and Rob Reiner (Mike Stivic) on the cover of *People Weekly*, March 27, 1978.

**And then there was mine.**
Beneath the crested sign to the old Mae West estate, now
named Ridgewood Military Academy, stood Iola McNutt.
This efficient Canadian woman with strong Christian morals
was my new boarding mother.

Away went my very favorite Reds, Whites, and Blues: red trousers,
white boots, blue shirts, snap buttons, and Raggedy Ann threads.

*Away went my freedom.*

I was a gay, fun-loving child, creative and generous, outfitted in green wool Army suits, khaki uniforms, black lace-ups, and military bedding. Although I didn't know it then, if the experiment worked, I would be changed.

*Brave Cadet*, Ridgewood Military Academy, Woodland Hills, California.

There is always a moment when you pray this is all a dream. I looked squarely and questioningly into my mother's eyes, this woman who sang Stevie Wonder's "You Are the Sunshine of My Life" to me every day since the moment I was born. I wanted to say aloud: *take me home, ditch this plan, what is this all about?* —but she had already taken a hard hand in creating this day of no return, and her husband stood behind her, justified and insulting.

Indicating toward landscaped hedges that encased a well-used flagpole and an American flag, she mustered up the courage to say, "Cheer up, Honey, it's good here… See, it looks just like a country club." She was not purely cruel; without seeing it, I was being called to repeat, almost to the letter, what had happened in her own childhood. Upon her parents' divorce, she was sent to a convent with her sister. I was being called to the end of self and to the end of freedom.

Awakened by a sunrise military bugle call and the rush to morning inspection by the older boys, we lived a farce. Adjusted to marching, we lived as if World War II were still ongoing: the hard-cut military way of life imposed on children by the school's Army colonels and lieutenants. Present-day reality rarely crossed the threshold. Ridgewood was the last bastion for corporal punishment in modern schools. Exiles with a payphone to call home, who were we and where did we belong?

Ironically, years before her movie career, Mae West wrote a play about homosexuals called *The Drag;* it never opened. She had already been arrested for staging another controversial play at the time called *Sex.*

Mae West believed that gay people were born gay and vehemently opposed the belief that therapy could 'change' a person from gay to straight. She would become a gay icon years later.

How do we get through life knowing we were not right to begin with? How do we act knowing whatever we say isn't being listened to? What happens when we believe nothing we say matters?

You can see why some people want to kill themselves. It takes a lot of strength, trust, and love to stay alive when you have no new avenue to support you.

In recent times, the 'modern-day genius' fashion designer Alexander McQueen, whose real name was Lee Alexander McQueen, hanged himself in the wardrobe of his London apartment, nine days after the death of his mother in February 2010.

On June 8, 2018, American celebrity chef Anthony Bourdain died of suicide by hanging himself in his room at Le Chambard hotel in Kaysersberg, near Colmar, while on location in France; he was seventeen days short of his sixty-second birthday.

That same month, fashion designer Kate Spade died by suicide at the age of fifty-five. She wrote a heartbreaking suicide note to her teen daughter before she was found hanged at her New York apartment. Her husband Andy Spade and their daughter Bea planted a tree outside of their big window to keep her "magical spirit and energy" close to them every day.

In a public outpouring, Spade spoke to his wife directly as if she were still alive, "You were and still are my Superwoman.

I hope you know how many people you inspired through the example you set in the way you lived and the work you created. You were and still are my favorite poem. I can't tell you how grateful I am for all you have given me and so many others. May your bright multicolored spirit shine down on us every day. Heaven is lucky to have you, but know you are truly missed by us here on earth."

If you or someone you know is struggling with depression or has had thoughts of harming themselves or taking their own life, get help.

The National Suicide Prevention Lifeline 1-800-273-TALK (8255) provides 24/7, free, confidential support for people in distress, as well as best practices for professionals and resources to aid in prevention and crisis situations.

Veterans/Military Crisis Line (for active U.S. service members, veterans, and family members) 1-800-273-8255

The Trevor Project (for LGBT youth, friends and family members) 1-866-488-7386

Worldwide - Befrienders: www.befrienders.org

You trade in your reality for a role. You trade in your sense for an act. You give up your ability to feel, and in exchange, put on a mask. Yet, we are not made to be disappointed. What carried me through, time and again, are the words: 'I refuse to be destroyed.'

*Yet, we are not made to be disappointed. What carried me through, time and again, are the words: 'I refuse to be destroyed.'*

During the Vietnam War—when the conflict was really beginning to build in 1967—Winsome McIntosh was among the few American women with a degree from business school. Although she couldn't get a job in business, Pan American World Airways came along, and on one of her very first flights as a Pan Am stewardess from San Francisco, she flew American draftees over to Vietnam. Survivors came home on the flights back.

That experience—of being exposed to bringing 250 to 300 terrified young men, her age and younger, to Vietnam, and then bringing a group back who had survived for that year—has been with her all her life. During that time, she witnessed a vacuum of consolation, and it outraged her. "Some asked for a Bible, but there were no Bibles on the damn plane," and it was very silent all the way back.

Winsome desires to resolve the anger she had at the time. Although she was a Democrat, she voted for Richard Nixon "because he promised to get us out of there."

She has talked to a lot of veterans who have been back to Vietnam to see it again. "I'm now seventy-five, and I want to go back to Vietnam, fifty years later." A personal pilgrimage, she feels, will resolve her mind about the actions the United States has been involved in the past thirty years. This will give her the 'new eyes' through which she will see the country not as she did during the war but in its current beauty.

"It's a beautiful country," she says. "The animosity toward the Americans is not there," and she hears that the real anger is pretty much gone from that country now, despite intense animosity on both sides. The answer to why this anger has faded, primarily, is that several generations have grown up since.

Winsome could have been destroyed by what she saw on flight after flight to and from Vietnam.

But she, too, refused.

## Getting to the First Step

Since the Vietnam War (1955-1975), the rise of circular ideological speech in the 'post-truth' world carries much confounding language about what are 'freedom' and 'truth.' An ever-widening, intentional betrayal of trust in the integrity of our information causes a betrayal of each other, a silencing of each other.

We must battle words, ideas, emotions—anything—that suppress the meaning of freedom. As President Richard Milhous Nixon was driven from office in disgrace after the oil embargo of 1973, he confided to one of his regular interlocutors: "People react to fear, not love. They don't teach that in Sunday school, but it's true."

The keyword in Nixon's observation is the verb 'react' whereas the verb 'to act' is absent. Therefore, to be able 'to act' we must battle words that suppress freedom.

Hell is this distortion—the opposite of freedom. Before we can lay new bricks, we must remove some old broken ones. One of the heaviest kinds of bricks is confusion.

Release yourself from the language that traps everyone in political manipulations.

In the first chapter of American vice president Al Gore's book *The Assault on Reason*, he scrutinizes 'the politics of fear.' It recalls a poignant memory, the night before the 1970 election when Senator Ed Muskie of Maine addressed the real choice confronting the voters. Speaking on national television, he said:

"There are only two kinds of politics. They're not radical and reactionary or conservative and liberal or even Democratic and Republican. There are only the politics of fear and the politics of trust. One says you are encircled by monstrous dangers. Give us power over your freedom so we may protect you. The other says the world is a baffling and hazardous place, but it can be shaped to the will of men. Cast your vote," he concluded, "for trust in the ancient traditions of this home for freedom."

The next day, Al Gore's father, U.S. Representative and a U.S. Senator for the Democratic Party from Tennessee, Albert Gore, Sr., was defeated by the 'politics of fear.' In his father's speech that night, says Al Gore, "He stood the old segregationist slogan on its head and defiantly promised, 'The Truth Shall Rise Again.' I wasn't the only person who heard that promise, nor was I the only one for whom that hope still rings loud and true."

### How can we do better, to act rather than react?

Our 'next act' in the twenty-first century is to act decisively against the darkness of the barren places of the soul. How can we do better, to act rather than react?

After forty-eight years of making the case for change through rule of law at the McIntosh Foundation—one of the most respected private foundations dealing with the environment and public interest law—Winsome McIntosh notes emphatically that "if you can affect laws in twenty-seven countries, you can really leverage; it's a tremendous tool when all else fails."

The Constitution of the United States is basically a solid document. Winsome discerns that "it always rights itself somewhere along the timespan," but how it is interpreted and used is the problem. "The biggest issue in this country is the influence of money in politics; our political system has basically become corrupted by money—who can buy this on both sides, liberal and conservative." It could easily be handled and resolved with campaign finance reform, she says, if more people realized how invasive and manipulative that has become on the population.

To illustrate this, what follows is a brief threading of three passionate leaders from the conservative to the left-wing—British politician Theresa May who served as the Prime Minister of the United Kingdom from 2016 to 2019, American conservative political commentator Glenn Beck, and the forty-fifth vice president of the United States Al Gore.

Each speaks, with differing language, about 'freedom' and 'personal responsibility.'

We need not spend time discerning if their views make any sense, or if they collide or not. But I am making a bold claim: although Beck is confusing and manipulative, and Gore tells us why, both are missing the 'pain point'—namely, that love, not fear, is what we need to live with the Earth. The climate crisis conversation is packed full of proof and language that makes us angry, hopeless, in pain, and defeated. We must find ways to say to each other that we're not going to stay in that state. Simply put, we can use their example, so that in turn, we serve as our own street sweepers, to make some way, to clear out the debris for ourselves.

## Maximum Freedom?

The United Kingdom's Prime Minister Theresa May, in 2017, said many times she wants the United Kingdom to be the global champion for free trade. In response to a question about whether she wanted Britain to stay inside the European Union's customs union, she said she wants British companies to have the 'maximum freedom' to trade with and operate in the European single market. Wait a minute, please. Is there such a thing as 'maximum freedom,' and what is it? This odd turn of phrase 'maximum freedom' is pitched to the public by several figureheads in public office and television, utilizing elaborate ideological and evangelical ways to inform.

One of them is Glenn Beck. "Maximum Freedom, Maximum Responsibility" is the title of a twelve-minute television segment the American conservative political commentator, radio host, and television producer gave in March 2013. *The Glenn Beck Program* produced classroom lessons for Americans that say freedom is about self-reliance or autonomy. The exhaustive lesson Beck gives about 'maximum personal responsibility' describes "why freedom should belong to you." It measures people's desire for 'a new sense of freedom.'

How far and wide can it go—all the way to 'maximum?' He illustrates that "you can't have maximum freedom without maximum personal responsibility." The two go hand-in-hand.

He teases out the logic: what does freedom look like when there's no responsibility? He uses a teachable example: "Jack is really pissed off. It used to be God, but now it's the government to protect you. Those that want to control every aspect of your life, they will tell you there is no reaction to your action, and they will draw you in… in seductive ways."

Where did it go wrong? "It went wrong," he says, "because you were lied to. It looks exactly like what the global left has been orchestrating for years around the globe, remolding the world nearer to its heart's desire."

This educational television segment closes with a logic model that explains to the American television audience that 'there cannot be action without reaction.'

"Freedom really is action. You have the freedom to act. You have the freedom to light a fuse. You have the freedom to eat too much cake. You have the freedom to make bad loans if you're working in a bank. However, you have to take the personal responsibility, because with every action, there is a reaction. That's the responsibility part," Beck concludes. "When you separate freedom and responsibility… when you split them apart for too long…"well, then," he asserts, "we get violence and unrest."

Beck evokes the famous Nobel prize-winning economist Friedrich August Hayek's (1899-1992) essential notion that "you have to bear the consequences."

Indeed, violent extremism shows us the limits of freedom. In America, individual freedom is something people will fight for, on issues such as gun control versus gun liberty. We are aware there is a big divide.

On the other end of the ideological spectrum, Al Gore's book *The Assault on Reason* brands conservatives as "enemies of justice and truth," engaged in a "systematic attack on the role of reasoned debate in policy and public life." Bashers of the forty-third president of the United States, President George W. Bush, loved the book. Gore claimed to not be pointing a finger at Bush and the forty-sixth vice president of the United States Dick Cheney but "pointing to the cracks in the foundation of American democracy." The point of his book, he said on National Public Radio, "is that our nation is so shockingly vulnerable to such crass manipulation"—to lying.

Barry Glassner, a professor of sociology at the University of Southern California, argues that "fearmongering" is comprised of three techniques: repetition, making the irregular seem regular, and misdirection. "Using these narrative tools," he points out, "anyone with a loud platform can ratchet up public anxieties and fears, distorting public discourse and reason."

Alarmed by how confusion is sown intentionally, an impassioned Gore writes that "If leaders exploit public fears to herd people in directions they might not otherwise choose, then fear itself can quickly become a self-perpetuating and freewheeling force that drains national will and weakens national character, diverting attention from real threats deserving of healthy and appropriate fear and sowing confusion about the essential choices that every nation must constantly make about its future."

*What if, instead of giving into confusion and fear, we awaken to how we have been hurt for too long and are now urging ourselves to change?*

A crucial action, to things we need to flush, is to re-establish an intense self-awareness of these confusions. If you keep going with a computer that is already corrupted, it's only going to create greater corruption. You have to pull the plug, or discover what is corrupted, in order to repair it.

Flushing the psychic toilet is as simple as acknowledging that so much has been corrupted that we as people need a hard reboot. We must embrace the journey before us and banish the corruption that weighs us down.

Fred Rogers, the creator and host of *Mister Rogers' Neighborhood,* who dedicated his life to understanding the inner lives of children, knew best: "Honesty is very hard. The truth is often painful. But the freedom it can bring is worth the trying."

These palliative words are the first step to breaking free.

Are you ready to start the journey, both outward and inward?

EACH ACCORDING TO THE DICTATES
OF HIS OWN CONSCIENCE

NORMAN ROCKWELL

*Freedom of Worship* shows four women and four men, each praying in his or her own way; some with eyes open, some with eyes closed. Multi-faith people of different races are represented. Norman Rockwell's series of four oil paintings — *Freedom of Speech*, *Freedom of Worship*, *Freedom from Want* and *Freedom from Fear* are in the permanent collection of the Norman Rockwell Museum.

# Prayers

---

**Prayer is for everyone.**
Prayers inspire and lift our spirits when we are down, and they give us something to do. They guide us actively toward seeing what needs to be released, surrendered, completed, forgiven, and cherished. They also bring us into the heart.

Prayers are a way of seeing human truth. Nobody better understood this than New York-born journalist C. L. Sulzberger (1912-1993), who welcomed *all* to prayers. His self-avowed atheism did not blind him to all that prayers have been and are, and it helps us see just how much prayers vary. Sulzberger enriches us, even now, drawing on his intimate knowledge of the human condition.

"One does not have to believe in God to respect godliness," he writes. A member of the family that owns and has controlled *The New York Times* since 1896 and an internationally known columnist working out of Paris, France, he was *The New York Times'* lead foreign correspondent during the 1940s and 1950s.

Atheism is "not necessarily intolerant a non-belief," he wrote, asserting that "atheism does not preclude knowledge of and respect for religion or friendship with the most religious of one's fellows, even the theologians of our time." During his life, he was on close terms with priests, patriarchs, rabbis, Islamic muftis and philosophers, and Oriental prelates, "some fascinating, some dour, some visionary, some pragmatic."

"It is not necessary to accept theism in order to admire the methodology of virtue," he imparted. Prayers, for Sulzberger, were not only a lifelong fascination but the ultimate expressions of human feeling, whispered or exclaimed by men and women in moments of supreme triumph, defeat, illumination, passion, or despair.

People are inclined to pray, C. L. Sulzberger writes, "For everything and out of every motive: out of fear because they are terrified of dying or its consequence, to arouse combative spirit of martial confidence during war, out of despair, for mercy, in request of solace or of special favors, and sometimes out of sheer love, exuberance or reverence." He saw unity and inclusiveness in the diversity of people's prayers. "Prayers, inherently, are human truth. They expose that stark-naked fellow, the soul."

So often, too, prayers and petitions are for immediate help and freedom from alcohol and drugs, or the obvious problem as it appears—sex, food, money, co-dependency. However, freedom from the bondage of self (as 'self' is the problem and the drugs and alcohol are a symptom) is the real issue.

You have to renounce your first enemy—anger. Anger in the heart is anger in the body. There comes a day when it is time to start watching your thoughts and seeing what is in the heart.

Theophan the Recluse (1815-1894), known in the world as George Govorov, observes that 'the prayer of the heart' is not only prayer of the soul and spirit but also of the body. The body has also a positive role to play in the work of prayer. He summarized three main degrees of prayer: (1) oral or bodily prayer, of the lips and tongue; (2) prayer of the mind, of the intellect or brain; and (3) prayer of the heart, or 'the mind of the heart.'

He said, "You must pray not only with words but with the mind, and not only with the mind but with the heart, so that the mind understands and sees clearly what is said in words, and the heart feels what the mind is thinking. All of these together constitute real prayer."

When people in the West speak of the heart, he wrote, they usually mean the emotions and affections, but in the Bible, "The heart* has a far wider connotation. It is the primary organ of man's being, whether physical or spiritual; it is the centre of life, the determining principle of all our activities and aspirations. As such, the heart obviously includes the affections and aspirations, but it also includes much else

---

* *The Art of Prayer: An Orthodox Anthology* (first published Russia in 1936 and published again in English thirty years later)—concerned with the meaning and practice of prayer—reaffirms that alongside the elements of spirit, soul, and body, there is another aspect of men's and women's nature that lies outside this three-fold classification—the heart.

besides: it embraces in effect everything that goes to comprise what we call a 'person.'"

It is necessary, Govorov teaches, to descend from head to heart—to unite the mind with the heart.

You will be pleasantly surprised by how many ways there are to apply prayers.

The concept of prayers having many applications is not an idea isolated in centuries past. The Rev. Brenda Husson, Rector of St. James' Church in New York City since 1996, draws us in to see an important detail about a form of prayer.

She describes a very famous icon, *The Trinity* by Andrei Rublev, born in Moscow in the 1360s and considered one of the greatest medieval Russian painters of Orthodox icons and frescoes. *The Trinity* is his most famous work and the most famous of all Russian icons. Depicting three angels sitting at a table, the icon is based on a story from the Book of Genesis called "Abraham and Sarah's Hospitality" or "The Hospitality of Abraham." Three angels who visited Abraham at the Oak of Mamre (Genesis 18:1-8) are interpreted as an Icon of the Holy Trinity. At the time of Rublev, the Holy Trinity was the embodiment of spiritual unity, peace, harmony, mutual love, and humility.

Andrei Rublev. *The Trinity*, 15th century.
Tempera on wood. Tretyakov Gallery, Moscow.

"It's also a form of prayer," Rev. Husson proposes, while noting that there's something funny about the picture. "At the table for four, only are three seated; there's an open seat in the front." In the original icon, you can see where there was supposed to be a little rectangle on the bottom in the front. "There was a mirror there," Rev. Husson reveals an astonishing secret: you are supposed to look at the icon and see yourself reflected in that mirror, sitting at that fourth seat. "Because what happens with Abraham and Sarah is what's supposed to happen with us; what God intends for us. And that is that we are invited into the holy feast of love... we are meant to join in and complete that circle."

What this tells us, explains Rev. Husson, is "If you have ever been in love, or you've ever encountered someone who said "love," you know that it's all that they talk about, sometimes ad infinitum! Because love will not be contained." This brings us to the prayer of the icon, showing us we are not doomed to forever hide. We have a seat at the table.

> *This brings us to the prayer of the icon, showing us we are not doomed to forever hide. We have a seat at the table.*

In the everyday world, art historian William Henry distinguishes that when people hear the word 'icon' they often think of a celebrity or a star: "Iconic means very famous, super successful. Awesomer. Timeless. A brand." In the spiritual world, however, "icons are images that function as sacred mirrors or portals to the divine." They show us "the way to becoming Awesomer. Stars. Shining Ones." Our world and the 'spiritual world' are opened to each other through the icon.

To guide us in seeing how varied prayers are, here is a tasting of C.L. Sulzberger's remarkable, joyous pantheon. For more than four decades, he collected selections that struck him as memorable or poignant. With more than 250 references to world leaders from antiquity to the current century, his final book *Go Gentle Into the Night,* published in 1976, is a feast-for-the-ages. This breathtaking tour de force allows everyone a way into prayers—from war and combat to love and awe; from solace to despair; and ultimately, death and dying.

When human experiences are "of the sad or negative variety, or when there is a craving for benefit or merely an adoring of the beautiful," he wrote, "most men have developed the habit of praying in appreciation, or in fear, or in desire. These expressions are often among the loveliest of man's creations, uttered either directly or indirectly for man's own solace on the all-too-brief road between the poles of pain."

Excerpts from Sulzberger's 'uncommon prayers' are united (regardless of individual credo) by the intrinsic quality of their content:

> Emanual Swedenborg, **a Swedish scientist, inventor and philosopher (1688-1772)** concludes: *"Truth is what prays in a man and a man is constantly at prayer when he lives according to the truth."*

> Emily Dickenson, **an American poet (1830-1886)** writes with delicate pathos: *"Prayer is the little implement through which men reach when presence is denied them."*

> Ralph Waldo Emerson, **an American essayist, poet and philosopher (1803-1882)**, touched with New England practicality, assumes: *"No man ever prayed heartily without learning something."*

Seneca, **the Roman Stoic statesman and dramatist (4 BC-AD 65)** decides: *"Fear drives the wretched to prayer."*

The New Testament Book of Matthew argues, like contemporary advertising: *"All things, whosoever ye shall ask in prayer, believing, ye shall receive."*

Islam's Koran includes in its daily quintuple rites of praying *"a form of healthy exercise, the physical reflection of devotion."*

Geoffrey Chaucer, **the English poet and author (1340s-1400)**, best known for *The Canterbury Tales*, suggests: *"Whoso will pray, he must be fast and clean. And fat his soul and make his body lean."*

François Fénelon, **the French Roman Catholic archbishop, poet, and writer (1651-1715)** explains with admirable French analysis, that *"He who desires not from the bottom of his heart, offers a deceitful prayer."*

Juvenal, **the Roman poet of the late first and second century AD**, sensibly proposes: *"You should pray for a sound mind in a sound body; for a stout heart that has no fear of death."*

Pythagoras, **an Ancient Greek philosopher (570-485 BC)**, is enough of a scientist to be a skeptic, and cautions: *"Do not pray for yourself; you do not know what will help you."*

To which Seneca appends: *"Don't ask for what you'll wish you haven't got."*

Aeschylus, **the Ancient Greek playwright and soldier (656-456 BC),** often described as the father of tragedy, warns, as if from experience: *"God answers sharp and sudden on some prayers."*

Oscar Wilde, **the Irish poet and playwright (1854-1900)** sourly observes: *"When the gods wish to punish us, they answer our prayers."*

And Rabindranath Tagore, **the Indian poet, musician and artist (1861-1941),** admits: *"I quake in fear lest my prayer be granted."*

There is a Scots proverb that says: *"He has mickle prayer but little devotion."*

Gotthold Ephraim Lessing, **the German poet (1729-1781),** believes: *"A single grateful thought toward heaven is the most complete prayer."*

Juvenal recommends: *"Leave it to the gods to decide what is best for us and most suitable to our circumstances."*

Menander, **a Greek dramatist and the best-known representative of Athenian New Comedy (342-290 BC),** restrains himself; he recalls: *"Let not that happen which I wish, but that which is right."*

The lusty François Rabelais, **a French Renaissance writer, physician, and Renaissance humanist (1480s-1550s),** writes: *"A short prayer enters heaven; a long drink empties the can."*

And Ovid, **the Roman poet who lived (43 BC-17 AD) during the reign of Augustus,** ruefully put a period to the argument: *"Do not waste time in praying."*

For atheists such as C. L. Sulzberger, who *"simply cannot, in all honesty, have recourse to others than himself,"* recommends only these simple words of Juvenal:

*"Prayer for a brave heart, which does not fear death, which places a long life last among the gifts, of nature, which has the power to endure any trials, rejects anger, discards desire."*

By discovering something new about prayers, an element of life, the ability to see into the heart, is restored.

Prayers assist in finding balance every step of the way. They restore imagination and hope, especially when we feel lost or downtrodden. They help us remain vulnerable and open.

Prayers are a living attitude. They are more than an entreaty, a wish to be fulfilled. Through my own wandering, I have discovered that prayers are journeys unto themselves, a way to pause, a desire to find ways of doing life.

# Breaking Free

Zhang Xiaogang. *Mother and Son No. 1*, 2006.
Oil on canvas. 160 cm × 200 cm (63" × 78-3/4").

Provided by Zhang Xiaogang, courtesy Pace Gallery.

Among the most important contemporary painters
in China, Zhang Xiaogang was born in 1958 into a
middle-class household. When the Cultural Revolution
began in 1966, his parents were forced to give up their
government posts and to leave Zhang and his three
brothers behind. Zhang's *Bloodline* series combines the
poignancy of old photographs—lost moments in time—
that he discusses in this excerpt from an interview about
his work (original language Mandarin): "*It was 1994
when this work became the starting point of a series of
paintings. It was simply triggered by the discovery of an
old family photo which made me wonder why the photo
touched me so much. So many things are embodied in
history that we have neglected in the past. When I looked
at the family photo, I saw my parents in their youth which
contrasted with ours, and I was deeply moved.*"

I landed in Inner Mongolia in 2008, a vast region of China north of the capital city Beijing, to work on sustainability and reforestation along with some of the country's finest foresters, businessmen, and government officials dedicated to China's environmental progress. A sumptuous welcome lunch was set. Amidst pleasant table conversation, my business partner was keen to invite me to her room for tea.

When I arrived an hour later, the water kettle was quiet. She paced the floor, and without any words, her tempo quickened. "Tell me, what have you done?"

I was innocent as a church mouse.

"What have you done to your heart?" She raised her voice a full measure higher. "I hate saying it, but who do you think you are coming to China to work on sustainability? You honestly think you have the right to help others? The way you have been treating yourself, you have no power whatsoever to help anyone. What have you done?" And then she belted: "Do you think I like doing this? Not for a moment, and now, I'm getting angry that you are making me do it."

What did she mean? What had I done to myself that made me unworthy of helping others heal? I had come to China to help others with a strong moral direction.

I knew, without her saying so, that she spoke of the state of my spirit and not some external crime.

In my unseen sexual life, there had been a period where instead of pretending to 'date,' I joined the mainstream routine of having sex with multitudes of strangers who abound in online profiles. Procuring casual sex on the internet is something people do nowadays. It's replaced the old-fashioned conversation you get by going to a bar. Online, however, we are all groping in the dark. Love was absent from my true self, and I had thrown myself out with the garbage.

Under false pretenses, I thought I wanted people to like me, to approve. I developed an extraordinary ability to make bad times look good. Labeling myself an 'environmentalist' was just one of my many methods for becoming a false container. There resided the reality that I was living with my dark side.

Determined to keep others from harming me, I was harming myself.

*Maybe this is what married people do,* I joked to myself, feeling trapped by a strong and angry woman. Aloud, I asked her, "Do you know what poverty is like?"

"No, I don't think I do," she said.

I felt, defensively, that she was like other well-connected European elitists who wanted to improve the lives of the poor in a nation of many. The problem I faced, in this moment, was that I saw myself now as the poor one. *This is how it feels to be poor,* I thought, *unable to help oneself.*

She could see the grief, but I believed she did not know the poverty of spirit I knew. Only I could know that, but I never let it touch me for fear of being incinerated.

After longer acquaintance, I learned from her how to get stronger and break free of my grief, my poverty. Frequently, she mentored, "Your intuition is good, but your 'knowing' needs to get stronger." She did not refer to factual knowledge, languages, or memory, not to the rational, objective, and structured side of the path governing initiation known as 'the road to God.' What she described was an application of spiritual knowledge in the physical world. This is the other kind of 'knowing,' of healing, therapy, remedies. It is the kind of knowing that is an inexplicable revelation of spiritual truths in which you 'know' something with absolute certainty. This isn't created willfully.

Another side to her, the one that was challenging me to not be poor, was six years of deep spiritual training she and her family undertook as landowners and land-healers, rather than as exploiters. This was her time, now in China, to use that training to help restore the land; she needed me to be strong, not weak.

An almost angelic self-searching overtook me during that crucial conversation in her hotel room. I utterly could not identify what it was she was talking about. In my heart, I felt ready to be useful in China, or otherwise, why in Heaven's name would I be here?

She railed with escalating fury, "You know what? You find a way to be one-thousandth of a degree off, and you get away, you escape. You're a master of escape. I have never met anyone as tricky as you in my life!" Her body had anchored to the elements. "I can break through to people, but you are the hardest. You are lying. You know the truth. If you can't have that, then go back home to the USA; let them beat you up some more until you are ready. You are not prepared to serve others, or the planet, and definitely not here in China."

After several tense minutes, I spoke. "I'm enough of a gentleman to avoid hurting others. Maybe, how I test my own strength is against myself."

She admitted that while there was truth in what I said, this explanation was inadequate.

For the first time ever in my life, my heart physically responded. It was a soft but precise jump, like that of a leaping frog. The Three Gorges Dam that impounds China's Yangtze River, about 1,600 kilometers west of Shanghai, is the largest dam in the world. That's the size of the well that broke inside me. I snapped, bursting into supernatural crying.

"That's good," she said, still sterile, without her recognizable empathy. "The heart needs a good cry now and then."

Compassion and a friendly empathy returned to her eyes, but she remained firm as she transmitted a series of most healing words. "I am speaking for your Heart now. Your Heart will forgive you this time. But you must promise your Heart never to do it again. It will not forgive you the next time."

She lit a Cuban cigar; smoke rose. "Come, let's go have a walk in Beijing."

That walk began my journey to freedom. That day, I began to realize that grief, so long buried inside me, had become visible. Subtle but enough for someone else to see.

Once that internal grief started to leak out, I did not yet see there would be a long journey of steps ahead that would take me away from that version of myself. This challenge to forgive myself worked for the moment, tapering the weakness in me; but the self-forgiveness didn't last. The world didn't get any better, and neither did I. My efforts to change the world around me soon ceased completely because a 'familiar but old pain,' as Kathy Eldon says, was tucked away in my soul. I was not a hypocrite for not being willing to change myself. I did not know how to break free in my soul.

Kathy's life story reveals what I'd begun to learn in Beijing: that the only way out of agony is to transform it into something positive.

## Escape from Grief:
## Through the Gates of Death

When Kathy Eldon came into my life in 1997, four years after the death of her son Dan Eldon, she had succeeded in coming all the way through the pain to a positive outcome. She even said to CNN: "I think one of the most important things Dan would have said to kids all over the world is you may only dance for a short time. His dance has been very short indeed. But he would've said, 'You choose your dance, you choose your music for your dance. You dance proudly. You dance with incredible spirit and vigor and creativity and life and joy, and especially you go out and dance with love.'"

Learning to dance and live with joy was what I'd been missing back in Beijing, but Dan Eldon died doing just that at the age of only twenty-two.

On July 12, 1993, Dan Eldon and his three friends, Hos Maina, Anthony Macharia, and Hansi Kraus, were killed by a mob in Mogadishu, Somalia. U.N. troops bombed a house believed to be the headquarters for the warlord known as General Mohammed Farah Aidid. Enraged by a raid by US forces that wounded or killed 200 Somalis, survivors lashed out at the journalists who had been summoned by survivors to record the carnage. An angry mob of more than 100 people turned on the journalists who were trying to help them, including Eldon, a freelancer for Reuters. Eldon and his friends, fellow journalists, were stoned to death by the crowd.

After her son Dan's death, Kathy knew she would never be happy again. Her book, *In the Heart of Life: A Memoir*, is about broken things and loss, but the main message is to not give up. Younger people would appreciate that the author writes in such a way where normal day-to-day experiences (real, plain, not mystified) become harder to contain than one might imagine. One can be a housewife and a mother; at the same time, one can break free. That's the key: to become who you are without guilt, without shame, and even in the face of losses.

Kathy's attitude—about fearlessly transforming loss and even death into something positive—is intimated in British spiritualist Dion Fortune's 1930s writings. The universal experience of death is something no one can hope to escape. It is only a matter of time until it comes to each one of us and each one of those we love.

"What then, is it we fear in death that it should for us be a thing of grief and dread?" Fortune asks. She understands why we fear separation from this mortal world and passage through the gates of death. First, we fear the unknown. Second, we dread the separation from those we love. These are the things that make death terrible. But how differently should we set out to cross the threshold, she says, were our minds on these two points: "Let thoughts of love, not grief, follow that soul upon its journey, as sea-gulls follow a ship. Let us bid him God-speed and good cheer and look forward to the reunion." We must not fear, "for in that sleep of death what dreams may come, when we have shuffled off this mortal coil?"

Kathy had not yet learned what Fortune says we must embrace: to not fear.

A picture of a caged bird is on the cover of Kathy's memoir. Nobody was putting Kathy in a cage exactly. "I created the cages around me. That's a horrifying thing," she says. Ironically, it was not only the sudden murder of her son Dan that nearly destroyed Kathy Eldon. In 1988, she was in a state of total despair over leaving her marriage and about "who she was, why she was, where she was."

One day in 1988, she awoke "filled with an inexplicable rage. I hated my life, everything about it. I hated my past and my present, and what little future I imagined might remain. I hated what I had done to myself, to my children, to my parents, to Mike, and to Jeremy." Mike was the husband she was abandoning for Jeremy, her lover.

Jeremy was worried about the state of Kathy's mind. One day, he picked her up and deposited her at her friend Angela's house. "Stop fucking running," he said to Kathy. Turning to Angela, he pleaded, "Please help her."

It was an absolute revelation to Kathy that anybody would care enough to do that, to deliver her to her best friend's house, to sit in the chair and to be told, "Stop running from this person who I didn't like—me—and figure myself out. Had I gone on another week, who knows what would have happened? That's where we started."

"We are intrinsically what we're thinking," she reflects. "If we're thinking negative thoughts, we get into more negative states than if we're thinking, 'Okay, I can do this. I'm going to do this.' And start to be inventive and creative and think about how you're going to get through the situation."

Trying to come to terms with her 'brokenness,' Kathy attempted meditation, massive reading of every kind of self-help book, and uncomfortable reevaluations but couldn't escape her grief. "I was broken. As they say, broken open," she remembers. "I wasn't excited," Kathy said. Her experiments with re-birthing had been quite enough, she thought. "I was finished with my anger, and anything more was unnecessary. Still, I wasn't sleeping, couldn't eat; I had a permanent stomachache and the bags under my eyes scared small children."

How badly she wanted to be assembled in a whole different way. "The pieces were turned around on the floor. To put them back together in the same old way, that's the definition of insanity: doing things in the same old manner and thinking things are going to change. It had to be completely different." It wasn't over, that period of pain. On her journey to healing, she had to "go and figure out how to forgive myself and love myself."

*It wasn't over, that period of pain. On her journey to healing, she had to "go and figure out how to forgive myself and love myself."*

That moment of utter despair led to a contemplative period. "It has given me the ability, the basis, for everything that I've done since then." She looks back on what became the beginning of an incredibly fertile time. And it really was a transformation.

One of Kathy's favorite techniques for seeing a way through, moment to moment, is Bless and Release. "It's good for whatever situation that's staring you in the face that's not helping you. If it's not taking you to more love or more light, Bless and Release! You don't have to hate them. You don't have to hate the situation or guillotine it. Bless it and release it from your life. That is the key to freedom: release whatever is holding you back, bless it, and move forward."

Most people won't take, or haven't taken, that journey to be open and more aware so they can become freer. They don't have to be stuck in grief and stuck in pain. The problem is they do get stuck there.

Bless and Release sounds like a snappy way to break free but not always, especially if your pain comes from reasons beyond your control. People who don't cause their own pain, but have their freedom taken away forcibly, are in a different kind of tough situation. It's not exactly possible, at times, to have the privilege of choice to 'break free.'

In uncontrollable external experiences, how can someone, whether younger or older, cope in the exact moment when something goes Blitz, Boom! Five minutes ago, they were doing great when something came along and took their freedom away. There are things for which we can't possibly prepare.

On the extremes, child trafficking, rape, bullying, refugee detention centers, and unbreathable air pollution all lead to poverty and the death of dignity.

"When you want to get into the drug trade, you need money to buy the drugs, but when you want to go into human trafficking, all you need to do is steal a child," the founder of the anti-trafficking nonprofit organization Innocents at Risk, Deborah Sigmund, tells people over and over. Among us, too, are those people who don't have parents; they are found in military schools, orphanages, convents, foster homes, and refugee borders.

To absorb it, a 2019 headline story identifies "Gaza's Abandoned Children: Palestinians leaving their babies at the border"—where "a worrying phenomenon has developed at the border with the Gaza strip that sees parents of children taken to Israel for medical treatment abandon their offspring in order to remain in the country as illegal residents."

If a kid, in any such freedom-depriving situation, raises his or her hand and says: *"How did I get kicked out of my own life?* I don't want to give up. I want to help others. I hear you. *But I don't know how...*" it's absurd to respond, "Never give up. Dream of some greater day later, when you're going to get out of here."

The phrase "Never, Never, Never Give Up" is bandied around too loosely. For it to have any meaning, it can't be amputated from the original lessons. I always took it to mean 'persist' and 'hang in there.' For people in abusive relationships, rather than being told to do something about our choices, we are sometimes discharged with 'tomorrow is always another day.' Hearing this, we start to tell ourselves, eventually, to stay right where we are in the status quo.

I have even had difficulty seeing a way to apply these to myself when reading the Dalai Lama's touching poem "Never Give Up," which extends to action verbs that take time and patience: 'develop the heart, be compassionate, work for peace.' Ironically, on bad days and even bad years, these words have made me feel I am not able or strong enough to work for peace; and haven't we all felt hampered by the ills of war, greed, and back-stabbing betrayals?

Sir Winston Churchill's October 29, 1941 address at Harrow School (one of the oldest and most famous all-boys schools in the world, founded in 1572 under a Royal Charter of Elizabeth I) broadcasts why, then as now, we should all buckle-up for the ride when facing crises bigger than ourselves. Famous for his inspiring speeches, the British prime minister of the United Kingdom (from 1940 to 1945, and again from 1951 to 1955) said "Never give in. Never, never, never, never—in nothing great or small, large or petty—never give in, except to convictions of honour and good sense. Never yield to force. Never yield to the apparently overwhelming might of the enemy…"

He meant, surely, having your eyes on the wheel.

But Churchill's speech, as it continues, includes an even more intense meaning than raw persistence: "We must learn to be equally good at what is short and sharp and what is long and tough. It is generally said that the British are often better at the last. They do not expect to move from crisis to crisis; they do not always expect that each day will bring up some noble chance of war; but when they very slowly make up their minds that the thing has to be done and the job put through and finished, then, even if it takes months—if it takes years—they do it…"

He was speaking of one thing: service.

Kathy Eldon, in kind, says that the solution to breaking free, from seeing yourself as powerless, is to find who you can help: "In life, often when we're at our lowest, we need to find a way to help others and find a way to serve. We're focused on our own dismalness, which is so easy to do, and we all do it, but when you can pull up and say, 'Oh, my gosh, you know, that little kid over there with no blanket is worse off than I am… how can I help?'"

The crucial concept of service takes us to another level within ourselves. It taps into different kinds of strength. "I've seen in friends of mine who are suffering from major illnesses," Kathy reveals, "but their resilience, and their spirits, often are fueled by the fact that they can help others. That's how it works." Do not be afraid of tackling whatever that pain is and committing yourself to an intended outcome.

Service is not the only key to breaking free. Kathy also identifies creativity as a major component of building a foundation.

She has assembled Planet 911 in recent years, a coalition that spreads the word around climate change to youth across the world using arts, music, and media as a way to protect the future of our planet. Because millions of people around the world feel silenced, subjugated, bullied, and "believe that no one cares," Kathy partnered with former Beatles star Sir Paul McCartney. His 2019 tune "Who Cares" showers youth with an anti-bullying message. "Maybe by listening to this song and watching this video, they might just think it's not as bad," Paul notes, "that it's the kind of thing you can just stand up to and laugh off and get through." The intention with this campaign, Eldon says, is to "put the power of the song to work and inspire us to show up and care—and let others know that we do care."

For Kathy, the only way she could get through the things that were perceived as loss was to transform them into what could be called a force for good. The loss of her son and the dissolution of her marriage—each painful event becomes a creative endeavor as well. "For some people, it could be a garden — you put that energy somewhere." For her, it was writing a book on grief, on finding purpose in life, on finding new love in her life.

In her book, *In the Heart of Life: A Memoir,* Kathy grapples with how we come to the point of forgiving ourselves and loving ourselves so we are more easily open to the love of others. Ultimately, she has learned, "The hardest thing is self-love. We block ourselves because we are so judgmental about ourselves that we cannot even imagine other people can love us; or that we are less lovable."

But learning to love herself provided other, equally important lessons. That self she couldn't bring herself to love for so long was more authentic and more compelling to others than she'd thought possible. In turn, "the most wonderful thing we can do for ourselves and others is to be authentic. Authenticity comes from an acceptance of ourselves; and with that, possibly even loving ourselves for exactly who we are. When I figured that out, or when I started not caring so much about what other people are thinking, I found that people were even more interested in who I am, how I am, and why I am. That really surprised me. My authentic self seems to be more of a magnet than when I was hiding behind something or trying to be someone else."

If Beijing was the catapulting moment where my heart first forgave itself and said 'yes' to listening to my authentic self, it was a journey at the end of our tree-planting trips across China where my heart experienced a transformation.

## Reactivation

Nobody could understand why my business partner and I mysteriously booked ourselves to travel utterly alone, 2,225 kilometers northwest of Beijing to Dunhuang, on the old Silk Road. Pressed for an answer, we were roundabout in saying how good it is to see and connect with what is old and original.

That raises eyebrows in China. What many people don't know is a large part of the Cultural Revolution's agenda was also the destruction of everything relating to traditional Chinese culture, officially called the 'Four Olds' campaign. Shortly after the launch of the Cultural Revolution in May 1966, Mao Zedong urged Red Guards to march across China to destroy the "Four Olds" — old ideas, old customs, old culture, and old habits. True numbers have never been estimated, but the incalculable damage to all of China's literature, scrolls, and other classics was massive. According to the book *Mao's Revolution*, 4,922 of the 6,843 officially designated 'historical interest' sites in Beijing alone had been destroyed. It is a wonder that the Forbidden City remains standing.

The Mogao Caves survived China's destruction of cultural sites during the Cultural Revolution of 1966-1976. Our Chinese guide, when we arrived, did not want to talk with us about anything to do with individual spiritual reasons for making such a journey, despite that it was her day job to bring wayfarers like us to visit the remarkable Mogao Caves, also known as Ch'ien Fo Tung (Caves of the Thousand Buddhas). An astonishing collection of 492 caves that were dug into the cliffs just south of the city, the first caves were founded in 366 AD by Buddhist monks and distinguished Dunhuang as a center for Buddhist learning, drawing large numbers of pilgrims to the city.

As the guide pressed us to move more quickly, I politely stopped her, explaining that we were here to stop when we felt a need. The caves are consecrated; left untouched, they are original, not in a museum behind glass but right in the middle of a great oasis at the edge of the Taklamakan Desert, one of the ancient world's most important intersections between East and West.

There we were, in an ancient site of Buddhist religious activity, that was also a popular destination for pilgrims as well as acting as a garrison town protecting the region. The sound of the Singing Sand Dunes, originally known in Chinese as 'God's Sand Dunes,' is described in the Records of the Grand Historian—a monumental history of ancient China finished around 94 BC and known by its Chinese name as Shiji—"as if listening to music when the weather is fine."

My business partner suddenly stopped by a small dark cave and seated herself at the entrance. Within a few minutes, she started to sing. She said softly; this was the first time she had sung aloud since she was sixteen. Yes, this was a moment of supreme grace, a voice returning after having been cut-off by a family trauma so severe it prevented her from producing the beautiful sound of music.

As she sat at the cave's entrance, I went inside with a flashlight and found, to my astonishment, that the wall paintings of this cave were of women sitting in gardens with their musical instruments hanging on the branches of the trees. I turned to my business partner, who by now had become my great friend, and told her, "There are all these instruments, mostly lutes, in gardens. I believe this is a cave of fertility. You can have your fertility back now."

She wept, also seeing for the first time that while meditation often instructs us that energy comes down through the top of the head, for women and for music, it can come up, too, from the base of the body.

Cave after cave, we found the inner heart of our authentic selves being activated. All we had to do was close our eyes and find it in our minds first. Opening our eyes, the mind had already shown us what was on the walls. We were, for the first time in our lives, seeing from within. There was nothing to do, not even so-called 'breaking away,' because we did that in Beijing. This place had been spared destruction. In the presence of 1,800 years of pilgrimage, there were not even such things to do as 'forgive yourself' or 'love yourself.'

We learned, together, what opening your eyes means. It means to unlock what has been locked.

In Malibu, California, twenty-five years after the death of her son Dan, Kathy Eldon's healing is complete. Most important to seeing that the 'first step is breaking free' is that she came out the other end successfully. Many, many, many, many, many of us…too many…simply don't. Many sit in recovery forever, give up, party on, remain pre-programmed, or simply refuse to see that what we truly can do is help someone else even before helping ourselves.

Kathy now feels "nothing but gratitude" for her son Dan's short but jam-packed existence. She posted to Facebook: *Bulging journals of Dan's explorations and adventures inspire me to try to live a 'first-hand' life; second-hand living, through electronic devices, films, or Facebook or Instagram amuse us, but most of us long for more.*

Now, Kathy can say to all those grieving the loss of a loved one: know that healing is possible. "With the passing of time and a renewed sense of purpose, joy can bubble forth again, filling even the deepest well of sorrow as we transform ourselves—and inevitably, the world around us."

As Dan Eldon said before he died: "The journey is the destination."

I had gained a golden vision in western China and Mongolia for the sake of the planet, starting a company that would gather people to seek solutions together. But that could not happen with so much sorrow in my heart. Each human is one of a great community, and no one person is sufficient unto himself. A true starting point on how to live, it was time for me to be a communal person, a fellow citizen. I changed and broke free from my sorrow.

After living in China, I got sober in North Carolina, separated from anyone who knew me, and I credit such isolation to the fact that I succeeded. Many don't make it. Many fail. I credit the simplicity of that place. A professional woman in Chapel Hill, North Carolina told me, "Stay for now; this is a good place to get sober." They tell you to do nothing big in the first whole year of getting sober. Learning to live sober means no new important relationships, no big new job that carries weight, and no moves. *May your life be free of highs and lows,* was inscribed in a book someone welcomed me to take home.

In Alcoholics Anonymous, they talk about the actual place where you 'got sober.' It's not just where you pause but where you stop. Because, they tell you, it can be 'life or death' to get sober. It carries gravitas. I cannot forget how hard it was to go to a meeting every morning at 6:45 a.m. without fail. It was the hardest thing I ever did. One sees little to no hope at that stage. One just has to do it. It was very alien.

I went to Canada. A huge victory for me; the healing process started.

# Prayer

*for*
*Breaking Free*

# "Breaking Free from Sorrow"

By Richard J. Marks


*Sorrow struggles against sorrow.*
*I petition*
*For unblocking the sorrows*
*Of my sisters and mothers.*

*Guide yourself*
*To the end of brute force,*
*With she who hears*
*All the sounds of the world,*
*Quan Yin, sound perceiver,*
*Beloved Asian goddess of compassion.*

*Congregating*
*Through Music,*
*Beauty,*
*Love, Guiding gently forward,*
*In spiritual redirection.*
*Neither the path of least resistance,*
*Nor most resistance.*

*There is nothing to 'do'*
*To give myself hope,*
*Except to see*
*The format is changing.*
*There is no more 'one more.'*
*No 'one more' to do.*

*Be gentle with your breaking free.*

# Don't Believe the Pain

*"Wherever there is a human being,
there is an opportunity for a
kindness."*

-Lucius Annaeus Seneca (4 BC-AD 65),
the Roman Stoic philosopher, statesman, and dramatist.

## Burying the Pain Body at Penticton, BC

When I stopped drinking, I was forty-six years old. I tasted the first little inkling of my willingness to stop drinking and felt my heart leap, much the same way it had in China. It said aloud for the first time: *How do I do this*? My father, who always provided me not a drop of champagne to toast my good health but a full bottle or two of the good stuff, was a hopeless alcoholic. "I'm ready for the other half of my drink now," he would say to the bartenders in exclusive restaurants and watering holes. Although he died at the age of fifty from alcoholism, I was not going to make it even that far.

In my second year of sobriety, I went alone to Canada. A healer told me "Go to Nelson, go to Penticton…go to the Rockies!" She anticipated how a road trip into Canada's interior would bring me feelings of peace and joy. Okanagan Lake in British Columbia is slightly more than a day's drive from the city of Vancouver. Canada has a lack of density compared to the United States. I could imagine life here as a landed immigrant, freed from America's competitive self-serving ways, hopeful and eager to embrace "a new life and a new me."

Penticton, a Canadian city of 30,000 in the Okanagan Valley of the Southern Interior of British Columbia, is situated between Okanagan and Skaha Lakes. Derived from a word in the Okanagan language, the Indian name *Pente-hik-ton*, 'ever or 'forever,' refers to the constant, steady flow of the Okanagan River out of the lake. Applied by the Indians to the locality at the outlet of the lake, it means the stream 'runs on ever,' or forever, in contrast to other streams that dry up during the summer.

I quietly arrived at the first part of the lake where I saw but one lone man fly-fishing in the early morning. The morning sun lit up the water's surfaces, and I blurted aloud words I had never heard: "It's time to bury the Pain-Body."

"*Pain-Body?*" I answered myself.

There would be nothing normal about this trip. But what is a normal day anyway? To the outside world, what could be bad about utterly enjoying Canada's magnificent scenery in wine country? Always willing to adventure out alone on the seas of life, "finding Canada" (rather than "finding myself") sounded normal. Pressing forward into British Columbia's wide and glorious landscapes, I imagined the voices of new friends welcoming me to Canada here in the First Nation's setting above Lake Okanagan.

The greatest diversity of aboriginal cultures in Canada live in this region where there is rich and direct contact with majestic fir trees, ancient forests, river rafting on the Mighty Fraser River, and really good wine produced in the Okanagan. The extreme natural beauty of the ancestral rock of the Canadian Rockies and its ten major mountain ranges elevate the spirit.

These landforms are a most glorious backdrop, including Mount Fairweather, the highest coastal mountain in the world

at an elevation of 4,671 meters (15,325 feet) above sea level —
most of it within the Glacier Bay National Park and Reserve.

It reminded me that we need to restore purity in and around
ourselves. Encountering beauty can be terrifying. We want
to go farther in, but it's hard to not turn back.

*Encountering beauty can be terrifying.
We want to go farther in, but it's
hard to not turn back.*

The piece of paper in my pocket was engraved *Tiki Shores Beach
Resort Motel-Penticton, BC* on the letterhead. On that beach,
I wrote down and accepted my real aloneness: "I have many
friends but few ever get close. Hearts are here to love, to show
love and be love. But I can't build trust if I don't know how to
build a relationship. Trust and relationships go hand in hand."

I buried the paper in the sand of the lake, and I cried.

To my own real surprise, I discovered on Google later that
night, the Pain-Body is much more than a metaphor. It is an
actual skin. The spiritual writer and teacher Eckhart Tolle
put forth its meaning and origination. He writes that it is "the
accumulation of old emotional pain that almost all people carry
in their energy field. It consists of negative emotions that were
not faced, accepted, and then let go in the moment they arose."

Conceivably, this reveals the roots of pain can be changed,
whether you're an optimist, pessimist, or just plain clueless.

Awareness of the Pain-Body could be a beacon of light for people. Acknowledging a Pain-Body is a way out of self-destructive patterns.

Tolle's concept of Pain-Body is a force based on these patterns that cause us to unconsciously seek pain repeatedly, to create unnecessary conflicts. He was born in Germany, grew up in Spain and the United Kingdom before settling in Vancouver, Canada. He never lived in France where, strangely enough, his name sounds like the adjective *écartelé*. *Ecartelé* has two meanings. Etymologically, it means to be dismembered in four parts. This was the death sentence in the Middle Ages: to be quartered by four horses pulling you apart with ropes. Its secondary meaning is to feel conflicted, torn, ripped apart by conflicting forces.

Over many years of clinical therapy with his clients, Tolle explicates what takes place with the Pain-Body in *A New Earth: Awakening to Your Life's Purpose.* "The beginning of freedom from the Pain-Body is in the realization that you have a Pain-Body. Then, more important, in your ability to stay present enough, alert enough to notice that the Pain-Body in yourself is a heavy influx of negative emotion when it becomes active. When it is recognized, it can no longer pretend to be you and live and renew itself through you."

I had, as Tolle says we must, become aware of the phenomena of accumulated "painful life experience that was not fully faced and accepted the moment it arose."

But what is trauma for one is not for another, and there was a message for me ahead. Overlooking the fjord lake of

Okanagan that has been carved out by repeated glaciations, my inner thoughts sent me an uncompromising directive: *You're done here. Go North. Keep going.* But also: recognize and move forward from the painful energy forms of old emotion.

*That's not fair,* I argued with myself: I had found what I thought I had come for, a place to rest in peace and beauty. But 'wayfarers'—the Hindi word for travelers—must stay the course, so I continued northward, looking for more of the lake.

By the time two hours had passed, I had turned fully sour, like the Roman word *Vappa!* for sour wine. This was a damning rage. No one, not one person I have ever known, was spared. The cascade of insults was as gripping as a day of hateful debates in the British Parliament: *Filthy! Shameless! Stinker! Thief! Triple-thief! Damn you! Beastly idiot!*

*This may not pass,* I worried. *I had better not go one more inch forward. Something very bad could happen.* And something very bad was happening; what Tolle calls Pain-Body, which I had buried the day before, had been taken away, shed. The protective layer of myself had been removed. Have you ever had a raft taken from you when you can't swim, or felt your wetsuit rip open to find yourself pummeled in a cold ocean wave? So it was then. The Pain-Body had come off. *Where is my skin?*

Rather than seeking to shed our skin, or believing that we can, we are given painkillers, we drink, we lie. People don't want to 'get out of pain'...they like their pain! It's because it is their most familiar skin.

I was exposed to the full and total fury of my life's pain. I thought about every person who had betrayed me. Whether as a child, adolescent, or grown person, there was not, in this moment, one person dead or alive who had not abused my goodness, lied to me, left me, cut me so far down. Who did they think they were? My dignity was rising, finding air to breathe.

Three dramatic hours of cursing were like being the star of a tragedy. The first message my brain received was a mixed one regarding the forgiveness of parents. My willful mother, innately an artist, had dishonored herself; first in herself, and then in me. I have been constantly trained—required, actually—to take and accept the abuse of others; to accept abuse; to kneel to weak men, worms.

And I thought:

*No wonder I let everyone walk right over me, time and time again. The chipping paint of the old self is scraping off. I must accept that the life I have lived didn't work out. Too many times, I stood no chance. It's time to curtail my own refusal. It's the closing call. I realize now that all old support has vanished, with no new material—no home, no country, no job, no funds, no love—to lean against or escape into. In the moment of becoming whole, I feel myself evaporating in the midst of terrible aggression in our world. Decide now: if you are to depart farther into nature, into even less, into fine particles—smaller, quieter, slower. Cautious, now, very frightened by the shadows of people's faces, by their splitting apart.*

The Pain-Body takes time to get a grip on, but I began to awaken to the important role it plays.

## The Passage Of Pain

It is painful to see someone else abandon pain. When you love someone, the desire for a quick fix to minimize suffering is strong. Deeply concerned about my continued journey through Canada's interior, a family member became even more worried about my stark isolation, likely thinking I was on a road to suicide. "You have to stop this and come back," he said, sounding immensely fearful that this was a journey to nowhere, undertaken alone and remote.

But, lonely and far-flung, the Pain-Body left, finished as fast as a bee pollinates a flower. The negative feelings stopped. The anger gave way to humiliation, insult to injury. "Things have to change. Now." I knew this was not *healing* but *change*. Healing and change are different; whereby healing is a process, change is a separation.

*Healing and change are different; whereby healing is a process, change is a separation.*

Healing has many forms. In the body, healing is restoration of health. In psychiatry and psychology, neuroses and psychoses are resolved. In conventional medicine, we heal from disease. Alternative medicine or spiritual healing have established many ways using non-scientific methods. Traditional ethnic systems around the world have practices such as traditional Chinese medicine and Ayurveda in India, in Christianity faith healing, and in shamanism, we find rest and clearing.

Through deliberately not fearing change, we begin to find freedom. But what should we seek? The worthiest goal, the only goal, is freedom. As Jean-Paul Sartre said, "Freedom is what you do with what's been done to you."

In every step of the journey to freedom, you risk an immense danger of not getting through the passage of pain as I have described. It is at the stage of immense confrontation with yourself that you may fall into the trap of believing the pain. Here we find people who are suffering a myriad of mental illness, depression, alcoholism, finality, and feelings of abandonment. *Am I making mistakes? I feel a tired futility. Am I in the wrong place? I want the disease of poverty to end. What can I do?*

Stop, pray, and keep going. Don't regret, don't judge, don't over-worry. It's about learning to walk again. Press on.

# Prayer

*for*
*Don't Believe the Pain*

# from *In The Shelter*

By Pádraig Ó Tuama

"Neither I nor the poets found the keys to the kingdom of prayer,
And we cannot force God to stumble over us where we sit.

But I know that it's a good idea to sit anyway.

So every morning, I sit, I kneel, waiting,
making friends with the habit of listening,
hoping that I am being listened to.

There, I greet God in my own disorder.
I say Hello
to my chaos,
my unmade decisions,
my unmade bed,
my desire, and my trouble.
I say Hello to distraction and privilege.

I greet the day and greet my beloved and bewildering Jesus.

*I recognize and greet*
*my burdens,*
*my luck,*
*my controlled and uncontrollable story.*

*I greet*
*my untold stories,*
*my unfolding story,*
*my unloved body,*
*my own love,*
*my own body.*

*I greet*
*the things I think will happen,*
*and I say hello to everything I do not know about the day.*

*I greet*
*my own small world,*
*and I hope that I can meet the bigger world that day.*

*I greet*
*my story,*
*and hope that I can forget my story during the day,*
*and hope that I can hear some stories,*
*and greet some surprising stories during the long day ahead.*

*I greet God,*
*and I greet the God who is more God than the God I greet.*

*Hello to you all, I say,*
*as the sun rises above the chimneys at North Belfast.*

*Hello."*

---

\*     Poet and theologian Pádraig Ó Tuama lives in Ireland. A gay Christian whose unwavering message is about the freedom that comes with speaking kindness, Ó Tuama's beautiful and very personal passage from the end of his book *In The Shelter* intimately shows how he surrenders with sincerity every day. From 2014-2019 he was the leader of the Corrymeela Community, Ireland's oldest peace and reconciliation community.

# The Big Goodbye

*"Before you heal someone, ask
him if he's willing to give up the
things that made him sick."*

-Hippocrates (c. 460-c. 370 BC)

*The Parabolist* is "a male figure pictured from behind,
facing a tornado with his arms outstretched. Bartlett's
work draws from iconic images of rural America, and
the figures depicted seem to belong as if by manifest
destiny. The wide-open landscape and expansive sky
are secondary to the eerily lit figures and seem to
function as a stage for the unknown epic narratives
featuring Bartlett's characters. An element of uneasy
pessimism separates Bartlett's large-scale work from
that of his predecessors. A dark tornado dominates
the background of The *Parabolist*, threatening both
the figure and the landscape." - Denver Art Museum

## A Spiritual Spine

My sister's failed spine surgery at fifty-three left her crippled. Post-op, starting day one, she had core tremors 24/7 for one and a half years. Just a touch of cold air made her sweat profusely, hot and cold at the same time. Sometimes she changed her clothes twenty times in a day as the full-body sweats attacked with paralyzing pain. Her clothes would be soaked, her gait became slow and awkward, and she couldn't lie down for more than two hours, at best; no matter how tired she was, the pain awakened her.

"It feels like I'm lying on rocks," she declared as she was told by doctors to wait one year for these symptoms to go away. A year came and went without relief. Some of the symptoms were a reaction to the metal that had been placed in her back, and two neurosurgeons and a neurologist told her that the rod from the fusion on one side had come loose and was hitting her spine.

The fusion did make some things better but caused more issues then it cured. "The fusion is not fused," an orthopedic surgeon diagnosed, offering to remove the bone where the metal rod was hitting the spine or to wait one more year to see if the spine fused. Until then, the doctors would not remove the metal in her spine that condemned her to pain management and strong Oxycontin and Oxycodone pills. The consensus was her spine would likely never fuse.

When I began to seek an alternative for her, I didn't account for total hopelessness. In Los Angeles, I inquired into a unique proposition: two brothers who work together, orthopedic surgeon Dr. Leonel Hunt and his brother, neurosurgeon Dr. Gabriel Hunt.

Leonel looked at the X-rays and read a letter we prepared to describe the situation. When he called, it was to deliver outstanding but unsettling news: "The spine is already fused."

"Why didn't anyone tell me that in Oregon?" my sister asked.

"Because they're assholes," the doctor answered with a sharp rejoinder. "A spine only needs to fuse in one place to be considered fused. We can remove the metal pins." Removing the metal hardware was an endeavor that would take a lot of courage; we would have to fly to California, well knowing that nothing before had worked in her favor.

We are full siblings, seven years apart, who have never had a relationship. In this process of finding healing for her spine, we had to be partners in finding sincerity and surrendering. Despite fighting for her life in Oregon, she did not believe we could pull this off, and still, we went forward. Twenty-five years prior, the father of her children had died while under anesthesia. His death stayed with her as she faced the surgery to remove the hardware from her back. She was very afraid to test her own fate further.

I was a legitimate brother figure who sat beside her before they took her back to surgery.

An hour later, she awoke from the surgery with a guileless young smile. "Look, I'm not sweating!" That night, she was walking around, and the next day, she went home with no crutches, no longer crippled. The pain that had plagued and defined her life previously had disappeared.

Three weeks out of surgery, she communicated to an immensely loyal friend who loaned me enough money so I could stop work during the months it took to get this done: "I feel better than I have in two years," she wrote. "I still have a way to go, but now I have hope. I have twelve grandchildren with a set of eight-month-old triplets. Because of this surgery, I am looking forward to being a bigger part of their everyday life. Some of the strange debilitating symptoms I have had since the first surgery two years ago went away as soon as I woke up. This surgery has majorly improved the quality of my life. It is not often that one meets a selfless person who would help someone they don't even know. Thank you so much. I hope the blessing will be passed back to you one day."

Because of her healing and the blessing that allowed it to happen, she didn't have to kill herself.

When you encounter people who cannot walk or cannot breathe, remember *you can be the first to surrender*. I surrendered to my sister in her time of pain and need, and my friend surrendered to us both.

My sister healed on a physical level with her spine, and on an emotional level, we healed our relationship.

What is energy healing? It encourages and speaks to the courage to say goodbye to 'trapped emotions.' Body-oriented therapist Jon Terrell from Northampton, Massachusetts has observed professionally, for forty years, that 'our story' is the pattern of thoughts, feelings, and perceptions that make up our sense of identity, our self. We carry these stories in our bodies. "Energy healing is, in its most basic form, the healing power of touch," he says. "We've all experienced the power of a mother's or father's touch that erases pain and gives comfort. It's the most ancient healing method." Anger, grief, and fear are what he calls the 'big three' dark emotions because they hold the keys to healing and awakening.

Some of us live a sad story, he has come to understand, in which "there's a sad little boy or girl inside who never really grieved losses and healed." Some of us who are living an angry story are victims: "People take advantage of us all the time; we feel hurt and powerless." For some of us who live in a scary story, the world's a dangerous place, so we 'shrink ourselves and live a small existence.'

It's to be expected that people try to meditate, or medicate, their way out of dark and uncomfortable emotions. We may advance to a feel-good state while meditating or medicating, but Terrell sees his patients invariably revert to their "baseline state of consciousness." They're not really changing at all. But when those "dark, uncomfortable feelings" transform into love, the process of energy healing "frees huge amounts of life energy and awareness that had been stuck."

When I was in the hospital with my sister, just before she went into surgery, I thought to tell her about a prayer I wrote during my visit to the medieval Palace of Fontainebleau, fifty-five kilometers southeast of Paris. It is the only royal residence that has housed rulers for over eight centuries.

During my visit, I had located a small hidden chapel and a simple bedroom chamber, separate and hidden from the monumental, over-scaled public rooms of the palace. These were the private quarters of Madame de Maintenon, the true love of King Louis XIV of France. Twenty-five years of precision handiwork were dedicated to the making of hand-embroidered roses of pink and cream silk, woven exclusively for this specific room.

I had slipped my prayer into the one and only crack in the private chapel floor. As if Madame de Maintenon herself were writing the prayer, it sought for love to be brought back into the courts of life (nations, cities, towns, buildings, homes, hearts) where we dwell.

I read the same prayer to my sister as we waited to be called into surgery:

> "Beloved forest, lovers, mistresses, kings,
> queens, and wisdom borne in the past of all
> the elemental mysteries: bring peaceful PAX
> power as a return of God's light to birth now
> in the hearts of the world's true leaders; grant
> us the means, the power, and the love to flour-
> ish as God wills. My being is pure, born of
> the golden light, pure breath of the holy spirit,

water of man's origin, form of art to beget all our collective heart. May God open our entire being to wholeness, and in so doing, manifest the power of Moses in us."

It was only when my sister looked at the photos of Fontaine-bleau, that for the first time, she recognized the power in my belief. It was not the prayer, but me, that she saw; we became one. And I, in turn, proved for myself that we can change when we look beyond the pain of our own mistakes. It's a common thing one hears that we learn from our mistakes, we learn from pain.

But there is more to merely 'learning from your pain.'

All cultures have stories that reveal our anger at God as we move from hell to awakening. Or if you prefer, instead of anger, call it *extreme tension* between the steadfast faith needed to find the strength to awaken, to align with your heart's desires, and doubt: "Why is this taking so long, this test of patience? Why does it feel as if what's good isn't anywhere in sight?"

*And Hell, by no means, is stagnant.*

The Renaissance painting, *The Garden of Earthly Delights* by Hieronymus Bosch, depicts that there are many shapes to hell—and that in each and every personal life story—mine and yours—the manner of hell changes shape.

*No path, no plan, only loose ends. Again, the chipping paint of your old self is scraped off.*

Before you can serve your society, look deeply and thoroughly into the reasons you resent not being listened to, held down, held at bay, discouraged, abused, and disheartened. You keep pushing away a feeling of despair creeping its way near, as it does. You feel almost entirely unsupported. Admit that you have lost time, have been lost, have been wandering. I have come to recognize that hell is freedom corrupted.

## From Hell to Awakening

Stepping away from hell, from what corrupts your freedom, is a new turn in which the private and intimate areas of your life are subjected to even more massive changes and unrest. Feelings of security, protection, and a belief in traditional values are jeopardized. Here, you are challenged to break away from old habits or maybe leave a family and home.

In the final analysis, these dramatic events reflect the urgency of an inner transformation to curtail your own refusal. Freedom is not about fantasizing what the heart wants but about being what the heart is. It means knowing that not everyone you know or even love is coming forward on the journey with you.

*Freedom is not about fantasizing what the heart wants but about being what the heart is. It means knowing that not everyone you know or even love is coming forward on the journey with you.*

You will reach a point where you feel yourself going through an awakening. You look at what you used to do and who you used to be. "The real voyage of discovery consists not in seeing new landscapes," wrote the French novelist Marcel Proust (1871-1922), "but in having new eyes." It hurts your eyes because you realize you believed in and promoted nonsense. You grow; you evolve, and you stop because you no longer operate at that frequency. It is then that you start to realize just how messed up the world is.

You want to help. You want to heal. You want to make it a better world. This is how you know you're awakening a higher level of consciousness. Recasting yourself, how do you make major changes that make something seem very different or even brand new? There are certain emotions that you have to walk away from.

We say goodbye all the time with separating farewells. In French, à *bientôt* is a mini-goodbye (see you soon), *au revoir* (goodbye until we meet again), and *adieu* (goodbye forever), which is used sparingly. Adieu means To God and is the same as saying as 'go with God' or 'god-speed.'

This time, it's *Adieu to You*. Your Big Goodbye is not an adjustment or even a hard reset. It's a death.

'Goodbye forever' occurs, in certain Western traditions, when someone is dying. They receive the last rites. Or, when someone wants to change for the better, and saying sorry is not enough, church sacraments (called sacred mysteries) may release the burden of sins and challenge those people to have the same kind of compassion and forgiveness for those who sin against us.

There are many ways to say goodbye. They can be verbal, visual, or in music. For me, goodbye hinged on the symbols for 'where was Dad?' and was like waiting for a bus that never comes. The symbol of an empty car. The symbol of a man who gave up on himself so completely he disappeared from life before I could grow old enough to judge him.

He escaped, but I didn't. Pulling the scab back, the wound of the missing father underneath was untended, telling me that the final symbol to lay to rest was me: the symbolic orphan. As you think about the day that comes for a Big Goodbye (and it will not be the last), be clear about the conditions that are acceptable or unacceptable to you. Focus on the symbol of what is not going to return.

From the past, whether your individual past, your family, or the travails of war in your country—whatever that might be for each person, from there, you need courage to see the real letting go isn't a mini-goodbye. It is not a superficial letting go of emotion. It is a death, a hard stop, a final symbol of something.

My mother, at the end of a harsh breakup from a bipolar boyfriend in the winter of 2012, paid a visit to Ilona Royce Smithkin, a vibrant ninety-nine-year-old acclaimed artist who emigrated to the United States in the late 1930s. In Ilona's tiny flat above The Beatrice Inn, my mother hoped to be told what to do in the wreckage of her life.

The drama of self-inflicted wounds still raw, she wished, perhaps, that the older seen-and-lived-it-all woman would be a wise mother figure, a seer who could talk her through how to fix things.

"You're an artist, right?" posed the fashion icon, author and chanteuse, whose long orange eyelashes were handmade from her flaming orange hair. "Well, so am I. And it wasn't until I turned ninety-one that I had the worst year of my life."

Incredulously, my mother asked, "Your worst year wasn't until you turned ninety-one? Really? Why?"

"That's just it," answered this ultra-vivacious species of woman, who had lived her life fearlessly, fully, and on her own terms. "I didn't know why, and I had to find out. I call them my pain paintings, and I painted almost 200 of them. I painted it all into those canvases."

Unlike her portraits of great people like playwright Tennessee Williams, singer Bobby Short, and the controversial and highly successful writer Ayn Rand—all oils on canvas reminiscent of the Old Masters—Ilona's pain paintings were done "facing the bathroom mirror." The exquisite drawings are departures from her elegant nudes in sanguine pencil. The series of self-portraits, journalist Reva Blau reported, were done while in tremendous pain after a lifelong "head-shake" (a symptom of living under the terror of the Nazi regime in her native Poland) that had taken its toll on her spinal cord.

Ilona explained her outlook as she showed the drawings in reproduction: "Something good must come from something bad. I knew I had to rescue something good, something beautiful, from something that was giving me so much pain, that was so bad."

My mother is a beautiful painter of romantic subject matter—people in love, idealized female nudes. Many are in the glorious styles of alluring women conceived in pre-Raphaelite and Victorian eras; luxurious evocations of the seventeenth and nineteenth centuries like John Singer Sargent's; self-portraits of women in lace and silk; a whole body poetic of water landscapes.

But 'pain paintings?' The antithesis of her way of decorating the world with sprinkles, with sparkles, with the desire of mysterious attraction.

My mother was struck silent.

"Yes," the elder woman said with great compassion. "Paint your pain paintings. That's my advice."

When Ilona painted her last pain painting, her pain was not shuffled around. Nothing left to sour the pot, it was utterly completed. She now sees life as the gift it is. She always tells her students, "Nothing is so terrible as long as you are alive. There's not an iota of pain left in me anywhere."

I call this The Big Goodbye. The Big Goodbye isn't thinking about or acting decisively on stopping a train wreck.

It is 'Adiós' (goodbye!)—a familiar word that comes from the old Spanish phrase 'A Dios vais' (you're going to God, meaning to the Kingdom of Heaven).

The Big Goodbye awakens personal responsibility for conveying permanent change. When we forgive a debt, something has to pay it. For the Big Goodbye, the debt is paid by letting go of the old self; it is the leap to courage; the awareness needed in ourselves to turn.

How is this done?

See yourself as a living symbol. This is a very ancient way—the way that native peoples see themselves.

> On the nature of native symbolism, Marie Louise von Franz (whose brilliant intellect caught Carl Jung's attention and made her his 'right hand' collaborator on the subject of alchemy) explains the 'living symbol' we need to construct and understand—and say our Big Goodbye to.

> "A living symbol can never be 'resolved' (that is analyzed, understood) by a rational inter-pretation. It can only be circumscribed and amplified by conscious associations; its nucleus, which is pregnant with meaning, remains unconscious as long as it is living and can only be divined. If one interprets it intellectually, one 'kills' the symbol, thus preventing any further unfolding of its content."

Lakota elder John Lame Deer explains that the native spirituality of the Lakota is so rich in religious symbols that "It requires a leisurely journey in the imagination to allow the symbols to speak to the heart."

"We Indians live in a world of symbols and images where the spiritual and the commonplace are one. To the white man, symbols are just words, spoken or written in a book. To us, they are a part of nature, part of ourselves—the earth, the sun, the wind and the rain, stones, trees, animals, and even little insects like ants and grasshoppers. We try to understand them not with the head but with the heart, and we need no more than a hint to give us the meaning."

Here is my Big Goodbye, addressed to everyone I've ever loved. It is symbolic, yet a very real ending, a death that we allow in the service of our soul.

> "Writing a goodbye on the day you're going to 'die'
> isn't the best day
> to be saying things in the ordinary way.
>
> There will be no more words.
> No more laughs.
> No more people to have sex with.
> But wasn't it already enough?
> It has been enough.
>
> A child has enough words and laughs,
> never thinking about how to squeeze more
>        from the future.
> A child may simply desire to be appreciated or
>        valued: loved.

Please stop lying to people; my request is to speak openly
about being a person who has loved me.
You love me—you loved me. You listened to me.
I gave you words. I saved you. I saved myself for you.

Please stop saving anyone.
Your service is to tell people you love me.
You will always love me. I never hurt you.

You came to me wounded.
You came to me with love and anger.
You told me 'I owe you nothing.'
I gave you my love without remorse.
The payment for my love is that you cannot love anyone
until you speak truthfully about me.

I love you because my design is able to leave you
without ever asking you to undertake anything.
I would, in this life, find fault in you.
I find no fault, and now you can be free.

I did not come here to save you or chaperone you
                 with words, laughs or sex
…because I had enough of them ever since I was
                 a child.

I do ask you to relinquish your lies.

That would make my love worth everything."

Once we say goodbye and die our symbolic deaths, we enter an intermission. During this time, you will need to re-establish an intense awareness about what you know of yourself by asking yourself these three questions:

> *Do I think I have freedom?*
> *Do I know that I don't have it?*
> *How long have I been pretending to be free?*

Seeking answers to these three questions is necessary in order to re-install freedom and restore love to every situation.

In all instances, be sure to examine your feelings about saying goodbye. It is important to resolve them completely.

Now, look forward toward the bow of the ship, stay to the starboard side that steers from dirty to clean. The fork in the road has already been split, and you are free to walk away from any despondency.

There's your compass.

Just as my sister had to say goodbye to the pain she'd known for years in order to heal, so too must we let go of old, familiar pains.

This prayer written by Hermann Hesse in his last full-length novel, *Das Glasperlenspiel* (*The Glass Bead Game*), arouses us to see 'the freedom of goodbyes;' without them, we would remain slaves.

Hermann Hesse, writing about the individual's search for authenticity, self-knowledge, and spirituality, won the Nobel Prize in Literature in 1946.

In saying our Big Goodbyes, leaving nothing of our selves behind but our names, the hidden experiences that cause us so much pain today, will become nothing more than memories. We awaken so quickly.

# Prayer

*for*
*The Big Goodbye*

# from *The Glass Bead Game*

By Hermann Hesse

"As every flower fades and as all youth
Departs, so life at every stage,
So every virtue, so our grasp of truth,
Blooms in its day and may not last forever.
Since life may summon us at every age
Be ready, heart, for parting, new endeavor,
Be ready bravely and without remorse
To find new light that old ties cannot give.
In all beginnings dwells a magic force
For guarding us and helping us to live.
Serenely let us move to distant places
And let no sentiments of home detain us.
The Cosmic Spirit seeks not to restrain us
But lifts us stage by stage to wider spaces.
If we accept a home of our own making,
Familiar habit makes for indolence.
We must prepare for parting and leave-taking.
Or else remain the slaves of permanence.
Even the hour of our death may send
Us speeding on to fresh and newer spaces,
And life may summon us to newer races.
So be it, heart: bid farewell without end."

# Personal Responsibility — Relationships

Antoine Watteau (1684-1721). *L'Embarquement pour Cythère* (Embarkation for Cythera), 1717. Musée du Louvre, Paris.

Personal responsibility is about love. It's time to get on with the journey of humane and caring relationships.

This large painting by Watteau, which took five years to complete, depicts the allegory of the voyage to the island of love. The Louvre Museum invites viewers to answer for themselves whether love is coming or going: "Are the lovers about to set sail for Cythera" — one of the Greek islands that in antiquity was thought to have a serious claim to be the birthplace of Aphrodite/Venus, goddess of love — "or are they returning from the island of love? The question is still open."

The French sculptor Auguste Rodin said about this painting that "What you first notice at the front of the picture is a group composed of a young maiden and her admirer. The man is wearing a cape embroidered with a pierced heart, a gracious symbol of the voyage that he wishes to embark upon. Her indifference to his entreaties is perhaps feigned ... and finally, the pilgrims help their beloved on board the little ship, which is decked with blossom and fluttering pennons of red silk as it gently rocks like a golden dream upon the waves. The oarsmen are leaning on their oars, ready to row away. And already, little cupids, borne by zephyrs, fly overhead to guide the travelers towards the azure isle which lies on the horizon."

I was invited to a beautiful part of semi-rural Pennsylvania, roughly thirty-two kilometers northwest of Philadelphia— about a day's march from the original American capital.

This was my first home visit to a good friend, a successful investment banker raising two young children. Now divorced, she had a boyfriend, a retired cop, who said to her, "You're letting a gay guy stay in your house?"

The day after my arrival, she put us on speakerphone in the car. I said, "Hello, it's Richard; won't you be joining us and the children today to Valley Forge? It's my first time visiting the military encampments for George Washington's Continental Army."

He said, "Too busy."

I pivoted, "You know, I'm glad I'm here. I think we need industrial hemp in Pennsylvania, a big state. The farmers need to have an American crop that's healthy and profitable." I continued, pressing on about how great it is that Kentucky Senator Mitch McConnell and President Trump signed the Hemp Farming Act into the 2018 US Farm Bill that became law, unleashing a potential economic dynamo for American farmers.

I added a little more about what makes industrial hemp itself so great, currently used in 25,000-plus products globally, before he posited, "Richard, can you say these words: Make America Great Again?"

I said, "Damn yes, let's make America great again by having a good crop here that we can be proud of, that helps farmers in every state, and is a plastics alternative because we have to clean this place up."

He said, "You know, Richard, you're surprising me. I thought you were a liberal big city guy" (and he didn't say 'fag,' which was nice of him).

I said, "A good crop for Americans should be on the radio, all over Pennsylvania, because it's a way America can be great, and I'm glad I'm talking to you, too."

As our car neared George Washington's winter campsite, my friend, with her kids in the back seat, smiled. She said to her boyfriend on the open speaker, "I knew you'd like Richard."

I don't need to be his best friend. I don't know if I'd want a retired racist cop in my house as an overnight guest, but there is always a way to have a conversation, and who knows? Maybe he's not as bad as all that, I can muse.

The day after that repartee, I told my friend to think about getting rid of him. A convenient lover on the side is one thing, but being aligned to your own heart is surely the only way to go when you're in recovery. After a bad divorce, why choose something that isn't up to your own standards? Even a small amount that's bad can sour the entire pot, and I wanted to help her see, 'I'm careful these days to protect myself and watch for souring my own pot.' I wanted her to see that where we find our freedom to change into something better is in relationships.

Two major impediments get in the way of taking personal responsibility for our relationships: not paying attention to partisanship (in the family or community) and energy leaks (in the individual).

In 2016, Facebook exploded with emotion.

Donald Trump steered a wide turn into the US presidential election, making waves (and baseball hats) with the nationalistic "Make America Great Again" slogan used by several presidents before him. Vendors in California began selling hats that said "California Republic"—a blatant phrase of independence not seen before. Hillary Clinton pushed for Americans to be "Stronger Together," and those who wanted America to have its first female president rallied "I'm With Her."

In a critical election series that led up to the presidential election, José Stevens, the founder, with his wife Lena, of the Power Path School of Shamanism and The Center for Shamanic Education and Exchange, a non-profit organization dedicated to educating youth in indigenous cultures, expressed that:

> "The United States at this time is seriously polarized and consists of populations of people that have entirely different value sets and who want entirely different social structures. Is there a way of bridging this divide and finding

common ground? It is difficult to imagine. On the other hand, if the country were to break up into a number of smaller countries, we would still be living right next door to neighbors who most likely would hate our values. That is the situation in Europe, and it doesn't look any easier than being one big nation."

Unbeknownst to us, our families, our friends, our most personal opinions on Facebook were manipulated for political maneuvering. Unseen powers were illicitly harvesting personal data from millions of people's Facebook accounts without their consent by Cambridge Analytica. Facebook remained quiet, despite the work of investigative journalists who reported it. The first one came in December 2015 by Harry Davies, a journalist for *The Guardian*, with reports by various journalists continuing all the way until the scandal finally erupted in March 2018.

The scandal is significant for inciting public discussion on ethical standards for social media companies, but the personal consequences are just as major and real for families.

## When Things Don't Go As Planned

A quietly competent senior executive scientist, JoAnn Milliken is not a person disposed to flaunting her emotions or political leanings. A PhD in Chemistry from the University of Pennsylvania, she worked at the U.S. Naval Research Laboratory and the Office of Naval Research and spent more than twenty years in the US Department of Energy. She looked forward to retiring from the federal government, spending the next couple of decades in peace and tranquility, traveling and doing wonderful things with her family. Her social media pages were a virtual filling station of joy and proud moments with family, painting classes, and love of women's baseball. The eldest of eight siblings, she feels it is important to organize activities that bring the family together now that their parents are gone.

However, in recent years, her presence in the family has grown more and more difficult for her. A family of moderates, debates related to political and social issues had often been friendly. But recent political events have been causing tensions that threaten permanent damage to her close relationship with her family—a monkey wrench thrown into the previously smooth mechanism of her family life. It is painful to awaken to a new reality: a daily battle between the 'Family First' principle she wants to preserve, and 'To Thine Own Self Be True.' Being open and honest will divide the family. Influencers in politics are dividing even people whose families are an integral part of their lives.

Fraught with disappointment, JoAnn faces a painful dilemma with her siblings and their children: should she speak out in support of her own beliefs, or should she remain silent? She has come to see how her pain is not due to differences in political views but to an apparent shift in national values that she also thought were family values. She bears in mind that "If we are silent, we are complicit." Especially for her younger nieces and nephews, she has felt a responsibility to be visible. "The whole situation is heartbreaking for me," she despairs, "because our parents didn't raise us to be like this. We have a very close-knit family, but I no longer feel that closeness—I feel like an outsider."

Still, JoAnn has tried to put her feelings aside, perpetuating the generations-old concept that families hold together like good democracies do—fight in the day but break bread at night. "We're not supposed to judge people," she acknowledges, knowing we should not trouble ourselves with what others do. Do not judge, do not criticize, do not compare. "But those traditional values that were central to our family have been abandoned, and she ends with "I no longer have faith in my family."

For her to begin to heal, she has had to step away—stop trying to fix things.

JoAnn must see her world, and her role in it, differently before trying to do things differently.

So do all of us.

She wants to fix what's broken—she always has. She was trained to be a problem solver and that is her forte. With disappointment, she mourns she doesn't have as much faith in people as she used to. "I don't know what the future holds for the family."

Any sense of hope visibly unraveled for JoAnn, and in a moment of genuine grieving, she declaimed that "at some stage in most people's lives, things turn upside down, and nothing is as you expected it to be"—the unerring point of no return described by Susanne Bier (the Danish feature film director, screenwriter and producer who won the 2011 Academy Award for Best Foreign Language Film, *In A Better World).*

*"At some stage in most people's lives, things turn upside down, and nothing is as you expected it to be..."*

JoAnn wasn't just talking about her country—she was talking about her family.

On September 26, 2016, the first presidential debate between Hillary Rodham Clinton and Donald Trump, moderated by Lester Holt of NBC, aired on American television. By the third presidential debate, October 19, 2016, Donald Trump famously retorted "such a nasty woman." It unleashed the Nasty Woman Movement and Woke Women.

The term 'nasty woman' is associated with the goals of the Women's Movement through an inflamed poem recited at the Women's March on Washington DC on January 21, 2017, the day after the inauguration of President Donald Trump, and a day of worldwide protest. A line from the poem swelled with maddening fury:

"I know it is hard to look at your own entitlement and privilege. You may be afraid of the truth. I am unafraid, to be honest. It may sound petty bringing up a few extra cents. It adds up to the pile of change I have yet to see in my country."

Woke Women also arose.

'Stay Woke' derives from the African-American Vernacular English expression for a continuing awareness. It has gained widespread use as a political term since 2014 because of the Black Lives Matter Movement. Woke Women intended to be a new guard of social activism from all walks of life—in which educators, journalists, thinkers, mothers, and creators share what it means to be 'woke.' Journalist Cori Murray describes it as people "who are more than conscious—they're ever vigilant about creating a nation in which we all have a seat at the table."

On October 31, 2019, *The New York Times* reported that former president of the United States Barack Obama has expressed his "disapproval of 'woke' call-out culture." Mr. Obama made "a rare foray into the cultural conversation" by objecting to the prevalence of 'call-out culture' and 'wokeness.' During an interview about youth activism at the Obama Foundation, his remarks about young activists ricocheted around the internet:

"This idea of purity and you're never compromised and you're always politically 'woke' and all that stuff," Mr. Obama said. "You should get over that quickly."

"The world is messy; there are ambiguities," he continued. "People who do really good stuff have flaws. People who you are fighting may love their kids and share certain things with you."

"I do get a sense sometimes now among certain young people, and this is accelerated by social media, there is this sense sometimes of: 'The way of me making change is to be as judgmental as possible about other people,'" he said, "and that's enough."

"Like, if I tweet or hashtag about how you didn't do something right or used the wrong verb," he said, "then I can sit back and feel pretty good about myself, 'cause, 'Man, you see how woke I was, I called you out.'"

Then, as described by *The New York Times,* Mr. Obama pretended to sit back and press the remote to turn on a television. "That's not activism. That's not bringing about change," he said. "If all you're doing is casting stones, you're probably not going to get that far. That's easy to do."

In fact, JoAnn takes issue with Mr. Obama's characterization. "I love the man and have a deep respect for him, but in my view, being 'woke' is a good thing. It is what people do with 'wokeness' that is either good or bad. And if you read his words closely, that's what he is talking about—the bad actions that some people take after being 'woke.'"

Awakening the morning after the presidential election that took place on November 8, 2016, JoAnn struck a painful mood on Facebook.

*Now America is no longer great. It is a dark day in our history—the darkest in my lifetime. The ugliness inside the hearts of Americans has prevailed. Our children have been told that it's not only okay to talk and behave rudely, crudely and hatefully, but you can become President if you do. And our daughters—we have set them back by decades...today we showed the world just how fucked up America has become and how*

*easily Americans can be manipulated. I'm ashamed to be an*
*American today. Ashamed and sickened.*

Putting 'family first,' JoAnn initially resigned herself to having lost. Deciding to put her family first, she went Facebook 'silent' on political issues.

And then something happened. The world's women started to come out of hiding, one by one. In a stunning turnaround, JoAnn also re-emerged, on December 13, 2016, with an unexpected declaration on Facebook that her voice was not quieting but rising.

Government and politics are not everyone's cup of tea, JoAnn declared, knowing "those topics can stir controversy or get tiresome, especially now." But after much soul-searching, she decided she cannot refrain from posting about or commenting on political topics. "I tried and failed miserably, and then it dawned on me that it's like asking my cat not to meow. I devoted my entire career to civil service—to the Federal government, where elected officials, political appointees, and career Feds and contractors work side by side to serve the American people—to make our country and the world a better place. How can I not speak up?"

Her second family are people in government she has worked with, and she is not about to let them be sullied. Emotional detox is not just to 'rid' our bodies, or our lives, of what we may consider negative emotions, but rather to clear out the ones that have stagnated. The same is true for relationships that carry those emotions, and sometimes, the heart breaks when it feels their weight.

*Emotional detox is not just to 'rid' our bodies, or our lives, of what we may consider negative emotions, but rather to clear out the ones that have stagnated.*

Relationships and families torn asunder by a major shift in values, or abandoned values, are not the only ones that can break our hearts.

## Not Yet Healed

Visualize an emotional speech given twenty-two years after the death of a man's mother, on what would have been her fifty-eighth birthday. Now thirty-three, the man is a new parent, a person who looks forward with fresh eyes. A promising life in front of him. But for the past twenty of the last twenty-two years—the life he has lived ever since the day she died—he has dodged dealing with it by sticking his head in the sand, refusing to ever think about his mother. She was thirty-six, and he was twelve.

Staying silent, he thinks: *It's only going to make me sad; it's not going to bring her back.* He knew; he just couldn't put his finger on it. He just didn't know what was wrong with him.

The way Prince Harry had been forced to publicly grieve Princess Diana—and as a result hardly grieve at all—did the most damage, he has said. He didn't let his emotions "be part of anything."

Seeking help, he says, is important for those struggling with mental health, "not just for you but everybody else around you as well because you become a problem."

"I, through a lot of my twenties, was a problem and I didn't know how to deal with it," says Prince Harry, now a true advocate for mental health care along with his brother and sister-in-law. "I can safely say that losing my mum at the age of twelve, and therefore shutting down all of my emotions for the last twenty years, had a quite serious effect on not only my personal life but my work as well."

His brother Prince William was a "huge support," Harry says, by encouraging him to talk with a professional. "All of this grief" that he had never processed started to come to the forefront and he recognized "a lot of stuff here" that he needed to deal with.

Of course, there was a lot of stuff to deal with: two weeks before his thirteenth birthday, his mother Diana, the Princess of Wales, died.

* * *

A family in shambles, a public divorce, and attempts to discredit you would bring anyone to the end of their rope. Princess Diana told her closest confidante, "I felt really sad and empty, and I thought, *'Bloody hell, after all I've done for this fucking family.'*" The family makes it "chillingly clear" that a legal separation, let alone divorce, would mean the loss of her sons; they would become wards of the grandmother, while she would be required to live in exile abroad. She developed an eating disorder, bulimia nervosa, over a marriage gone sour; and her closest friends were concerned for her physical and mental health after five rumored suicide attempts.

It's a dangerous time in which she might have remained forever trapped and doomed in her own estrangement and misery, the Princess in the castle, without hope of ever having painless love.

In one of the longest speeches Diana ever delivered, the central message of her contribution to European Drug Prevention Week was a simple one: "Lavish physical affection upon your children and they will be less likely to look for artificial substitutes such as drugs." Known to be a copious hugger of her sons, she said, "Hugging has no harmful side effects... there are potential huggers in every household."

*Vanity Fair* contributor Anthony Holden profiled that Diana appeared to be delivering "coded messages about her husband Charles's personal inadequacies, given a cold and formal upbringing starved of physical affection" when she said, "Children are not chores, they are part of us. If we gave them the love they deserve, they would not try so hard to attract our attention...and children who have received the affection they deserve will usually continue to recognize how good it feels, how right it feels, and will create that feeling around them. We've all seen the families of the skilled survivors. Their strength comes from within and was put there by means of learning how to give and receive affection, without restraint or embarrassment, from their earliest days."

Ominously, Diana went on, "If the immediate family breaks up, the problems created can still be resolved, but only if the children have been brought up from the very start with the feeling that they are wanted, loved, and valued. Then they are better able to cope with such crises."

With the announcement of her divorce on December 9, 1992, Diana, Princess of Wales, was visibly reborn. She was free to live an independent life. For Diana, it was a moment of triumph.

Saving the monarchy (from itself) is what *Vanity Fair* has called "Diana's Revenge"—a hard-won victory over her in-laws. After a lifetime of emotional disappointments, and though separated from the royal family, she "fashioned her own set of rules in one of the world's strictest households." There was "a new bounce in her step, a cheekier smile on her face, a new gleam in those flirtatious blue eyes. Prime Minister John Major's dramatic announcement in the House of Commons ended more than five years of lies, deceptions, and pent-up suffering. At long last, the sham was over."

But for Harry, before and after his mother's death, there was no relief.

Prince Harry's story epitomizes how very human it is to overcome even a multi-generational legacy of trauma. The colorful travails of Prince Harry's youth as a bad-boy were sensationalized and documented in newspapers. The public grew to know him from one-shot-too-many drinking binges, nightclub fights, streaking, marijuana use, trouble at school, insensitive remarks, and smooching in public. Everyone knew he was over the top. But was he 'scared straight' when his father sent him to rehab for a day? Even then, his wild-child antics would not slow down.

Prince Harry's start to a solid healing didn't begin until he spoke with friends and family, and then a therapist. He realized it was the unattended, unresolved grief of losing his mother so young that was possibly crippling him.

Now in his thirties, Harry has learned that finding a way to be a role model and mentor can help heal the wounds of your own past and create a better future for someone else. "The impact of a mentor has the power to make society richer, happier, kinder, and more aligned," he said in a speech at the first-ever Diana Award National Youth Mentoring Summit. Twenty-two years since the death of his mother, Harry now carries her boldly to all of us with newfound clarity: "My mother was a role model to so many, without realizing the impact she would have on so many lives. You don't have to be a princess or a public figure to be a role model. In fact, it's equally valuable if you're not because it's more relatable."

It is important, for all of us, to activate beyond our immediate family and farther than our immediate context of love. The question is, are you able to relinquish all that you know—the entire structure of the belief system that defines and constricts your reality—for the chance that you may experience the perspective of your own expanded self? Enduring freedom does not come from outer circumstances but from inner liberation—the disappearance of the ego.

*Enduring freedom does not come from outer circumstances but from inner liberation—the disappearance of the ego.*

There is no more worthwhile agenda than to work at enlarging our emotional capacity throughout our lives. A decisive aspect of growing up is to be deliberate, not merely playing a role (training, jobs, spouses, lip-service), but rekindling how you always wanted to live your life (before all those roles took over). Today is the whistle, indicating that it is perfectly fine to walk away from self-serving ways. We can promote justice and love and live in peace with one another; we only need to stay with it and see it come to fruition.

The wisdom book *Oneness* by Rasha explains, "As you begin to release the constraints that bind you to circumstances you have outgrown; you will discover that the direction of choice is found on a road you must travel alone." That is true for a while, "But as you gather the fragments of the structure that crumbles around you, and you cease trying to make sense of it, you will come to embrace the peace of knowing the struggle is, at last, coming to an end. And you will experience a sense of sweet detachment from what was, and an openness to what is yet to be."

*Your gains in freedom (the opposite of which is hell), however you choose to come to it, will be for the world. When you expect and anticipate outcomes for all concerned, those outcomes start to become manifested as reality.*

This voice is saying: it's time to get on with the journey of humane and caring relationships. We have begun to move from fragmentation to integration when we start to treat other people as ourselves, rather than with the simplistic 'kindness' applied to strangers as charity. Allow that transformation, for as Dan Eldon said, when the 'journey is the destination,' your primary motivation changes from being all about yourself and becomes for the sake of others. Your gains in freedom (the opposite of which is hell), however you choose to come to it, will be for the world. When you expect and anticipate outcomes for all concerned, those outcomes start to become manifested as reality.

## It's About Love

For Tamara Buchwald, that responsibility is really all about love. When she says 'love,' she thinks of people. Even though she went to law school, her priority was getting married and having children. It's her reason for being. "I believe that you can only create loving relationships through bonding, and bonding is only done through time spent with someone."

Tamara died as a baby. Six months old, she was pronounced dead. To bring her back, they broke her ribs, broke her jaw. Her mother, who was never very maternal, moved into the hospital with her. "In the 1960s, you didn't do that. You would leave your baby and come see your baby. But she moved in." Her grandmother and her dad took care of her siblings while her mother remained in the hospital with her. Her husband, Joel, is convinced this made her who she is.

"Trauma is huge—so important," she says. "Up there with freedom and love. That's the problem with our society. We don't deal with our trauma. You have to feel the disappointment like you feel the successes in life. Everything—happiness and sadness, disappointment and struggle."

She holds the strength of personal responsibility up like a mirror to the life story of Elizabeth Smart. The fourteen-year-old from Salt Lake City, Utah, who was kidnapped and held captive for nine months, came out of it and let it identify her; she did not let it take over her life. Smart was abducted from her home at knifepoint, held at a camp in the woods and repeatedly raped. Since her abduction, Smart has gone on to become an advocate for missing persons and victims of sexual assault.

"That's a strong person," Tamara repeats.

How we all can come through to the other side of trauma, Tamara extrapolates, is shown in how Elizabeth allowed herself to feel everything and release it: "You have to let the trauma identify you."

*"You have to let the trauma identify you."*

Tamara learned about personal responsibility through an intermediary, an older mentor whose name was Guy Webster. A famous photographer from Ojai, California whose rock photography spanned 1964 to 1971, Webster left America in protest of the Nixon administration. He captured images seen on album covers such as *The Doors* 1967 self-titled LP, Simon & Garfunkel's *Sounds of Silence*, and the Byrds' *Turn! Turn! Turn!*.

Tamara remembers "He really was a child of the '60s. He had so many friends and he really believed in the whole love thing.

That's what it was all about. When he died, he belonged to everyone but belonged to no one."

This shows that we belong to each other. "Love," she fully grasped the year her father died, "it's all relationships."

In daily prayers, her family takes center stage. "I say thank you first, and then I pray. I thank God for the love of my life. My family. That's the most important thing. To enjoy this opportunity to live."

Having given thanks for your relationships, it is important to appreciate your own assets and liabilities. Quite simply, a progression for being honest should become a daily habit. What can you forgive each day?

A 'Daily Moral Inventory' every morning is a useful anti-vanity mirror. A stellar inventory (which you can adapt) has its origins in Alcoholics Anonymous. Notice how the verbs 'watch' and 'strive' are in interplay, and help us to see ourselves, literally, in our own mirror. As we become less reactive, our personal responsibility matures.

The *Alcoholics Anonymous: Big Book* says, "We grow by our willingness to face and rectify errors and convert them into assets." Character 'Liabilities' are what to 'watch for' that eliminate the negative. Reflected back as 'Assets' are what to 'strive for' that accentuate the positive.

# Prayer

*for*
*Personal Responsibility — Relationships*

# Daily Moral Inventory

By an anonymous committee

*Watch for anger, Strive for self-control;*
*Watch for self-pity, Strive for self-forgiveness;*
*Watch for self-justification, Strive for integrity;*
*Watch for self-importance, Strive for modesty;*
*Watch for self-condemnation, Strive for self-esteem;*
*Watch for dishonesty, Strive for honesty;*
*Watch for impatience, Strive for patience;*
*Watch for hate, Strive for love;*
*Watch for resentment, Strive for forgiveness;*
*Watch for false pride, Strive for humility;*
*Watch for jealousy, Strive for trust;*
*Watch for envy, Strive for generosity;*
*Watch for laziness, Strive for activity;*
*Watch for procrastination, Strive for promptness;*
*Watch for insincerity, Strive for straightforwardness;*
*Watch for negative thinking, Strive for positive thinking;*
*Watch for criticizing, Look for the good;*
*Watch for fear, Strive for faith.*

# Worthy of Love

*Peroration*

The first is freedom of speech and expression everywhere in the world.

The second is ~~the~~ freedom of every person to worship God in his own way everywhere in the world

The third is freedom from want — which translated into international terms means economic understandings which will secure to every nation everywhere a healthy peace time life for its inhabitants.

The fourth is freedom from fear — which translated into international terms means a world-wide reduction of armaments to such a point and ~~by~~ in such a thorough fashion that no nation anywhere will be in a position to commit an act of physical aggression against any neighbor.

In his own hand, Franklin D. Roosevelt's State of
the Union Address, known as the "Four Freedoms"
speech, proposed four fundamental freedoms
that people "everywhere in the world" ought to
enjoy: freedom of speech and expression, freedom
of every person to worship, freedom from want,
and freedom from fear. The theme of the Four
Freedoms, in which he identified essential human
rights that should be universally protected, was
incorporated into the Atlantic Charter, and became
part of the charter of the United Nations.

I was steered away from puritanical ways of seeing to spiritual ways, well before I found love. My initiation—into learning to be in contact with the mysteries of life—was not in a church, temple, summer camp, or a school, despite that we sang songs and sometimes 'prayed together' in all these places.

A month shy of sixteen years old, I walked myself up the steep steps of a tall and narrow Victorian that stood on Van Ness Street in San Francisco. My friend Edie Dushkin Soeiro, whose brilliant young son, just fourteen, died of cancer, paid visits to this place for healing and contact beyond the veil of death.

Its name was Amron—a word of Eritrea origin that means 'as we desire.' Amron, founded by a distinguished spiritualist, Norma Tringaldi, was the vocation of a healing mediator whose life in San Francisco took her to a very unexpected realm.

Unlike any church, temple, or school I had grown up around, I would come to know, in time, that its roots were in the ancient mystery traditions. People who carry the traditions of seeing what is hidden by the senses, transcendent of time and space, have been called by many names—some nice and others threatening—folk healer, artist, wizard, psychic, seer. Being a mediator, someone who sees into the unseen realm, has a succulent history as long back as time itself, often populated by a hierarchy of 'masters.'

But every now and then, someone comes along who opens the door for you to trust your intuition, to see common sense in your instincts, to help you find your internal feelings, to tune you into your own emotions.

Eager to learn about myself beyond the 'well-brought-up' boy I had been bred to be—an insider phrase we call WBU—I encountered a rarefied setting.

"It's hard to give people hope," Norma began. I didn't instantly understand what she meant, but one only had to open the curtains and look outside to see it in the faces of people, some of whom were our own high school teachers, businessmen, homeless, elected officials, socialites, wig makers, drug dealers, realtors, clergy, waiters, every imaginable human role-play.

We were young but not starry-eyed; the year was 1983, my mother would write letters cautioning me to stay clear of the 'plague' in San Francisco, and my best friend and I recognized together, saying it aloud: "We are the AIDS generation."

The plague of AIDS and weakened immune systems around the nation had first come into public view two years prior in 1981. At this point, the term 'gay cancer' entered the public lexicon. A year later, in 1982, *The New York Times* published the first mention of the term "GRID" (Gay-Related Immune Deficiency), which some researchers were using to describe the new epidemic. The term deepened the public perception that AIDS affects only gay men.

By 1983, WARD 86—the world's first dedicated outpatient AIDS clinic—opened at San Francisco General Hospital, and the Center for Disease Control (CDC) hosted a public meeting to identify opportunities to "protect the nation's blood supply from AIDS." AIDS activist Larry Kramer published a blistering assessment of the impact of AIDS on the gay community in the biweekly *New York Native*. The essay "1,121 and Counting" is "a frantic plea for that community to get angry at the lack of government support for sick and dying gay men and the slow pace of scientific progress in finding a cause for AIDS." By the end of 1983, the World Health Organization (WHO) hosted its first meeting to assess the global AIDS situation and began international surveillance.

In a city so beautiful that it is known as the Paris of the West, Norma would increasingly spend the duration of her life in San Francisco touching the worst fears—phantom and real—of men with AIDS. Her work, even as a mystic, was true pastoral care—an ancient model of emotional and spiritual support that can be found in all cultures and traditions.

Across Norma's large desk were spiritual books of every kind. I noticed next to her an assemblage of the Seven Dwarves' figurines, seven little mystical men who lived in a tiny cottage. Disney, the company that birthed The Magic Kingdom, and the masterpiece *Snow White* (created in 1937) where magical energies are utilized and mystical transformations take place, is responsible for how a majority of the general public has envisioned magic. The Seven Dwarves are widely known to be the "seven moods of man" (rather than "seven deadly sins"— which are also in the Snow White story). Norma added her own touch of magic by telling me they are also the "seven chakras," and Dopey, the youngest, was her favorite because he was the archetype of the Fool representing beginnings and innocence.

What we need in the world is magic, and Norma engraved on me these lasting words of practical wisdom for being on the spiritual path: 'Life is a mystery to be lived, not a problem to be solved.'

*What we need in the world is magic.*

Well off the beaten path from conventional religion (or even atheism), I inquired of Norma what are 'mystery traditions?'

Guiding and speaking with me about my possible life's path and purpose, she discerned I had not yet learned how to get on 'the wheel of life.' In the midst of this very new experience of meeting a famed medium, she described me as 'a diamond in the rough,' walked me to a bookshelf, and drew down the books whose 'nom de plume' was Dion Fortune (given name Violet Penry-Evans, née Violet Firth). "I like her because she's practical," Norma said, showing why even something as esoteric as ancient tradition and the 'inner light' of mysticism could be of help to me and others. "She wrote in an era where so much was hidden in secrecy," Norma explained. These popular novels were given for everyday uninitiated lay people to 'fend for themselves' against some very strange things.

"In times of universal stress, such as the present," Fortune wrote immediately following Britain's declaration of war on

Germany after Hitler's troops invaded Poland in 1939, "we find ourselves sensitized to things of which we are normally unaware, or of which, though we may know in theory, we have no personal experience. Among these is the 'group-soul' of the race. Who has not felt a sense of participation in this larger being, a total inability to insulate ourselves from it, however we might try?"

Fortune recognized that, then as now, we must push ourselves away from all forces of self-tyranny; and her encouragement was that we already know what they are.

Amron's existence faded when Norma died, and its memory of esoteric knowledge gently washed away along with the AIDS era and all the hopeless people who died in it. I have had to accept, despite that my desire is for self-healing and to be a doorway for anyone with enough willingness and guidance, there are times where these desires are just not possible. Some of us leave the planet, don't rebound, succumb to experiences in which self-healing cannot even begin. Norma, who lived amid monumental historical crisis, never made it to the Age of the Internet— the big yearbook in the sky where everything is recorded—and when she died, there was no memoir or book, no souvenir of her life.

She was a spiritual guide whose figure can still be traced in the next generations of fearless women and men who pay respect to the High Priestess, the archetype of intuition who meets common sense and practical work.

It is perplexing to identify the 'real us' in life because we are a complex pattern of memories, aspirations and actions that make up our characters, and until our deaths, that pattern is carried by the atoms of our body. Norma's allegory about what stands in the way of giving and having hope is central to our building self-worth in a society based on highlighting our shortcomings. Comparing ourselves to what is happening around us suggests a 'fix' will help us feel worthy. But to begin to gain freedom, we must replace the feeling of control with an appetite for fearlessly obtaining self-worth. We can make ourselves better by choosing to not live by external measures of ourselves.

If you have difficulty seeing yourself as worthy of love— accepting yourself as you are right now may not actually be the best thing to do.

## Lessons from exposure to violence

Our Veterans, Soldiers, and Families of Soldiers have a particularly fitting reason for healing, and to break free from what others may view as a presumed hell (which is, remember, freedom that has been taken away or corrupted).

Among narratives that were the most difficult for former military psychiatrist Nancy B. Black, MD, Colonel, US Army, Retired, were some that were also the hardest experiences for the Servicemembers she cares for, when they described the events and their injuries that bring them to her office. Two had been drivers when serving in the Iraq War. No one knows with certainty how many were killed and wounded in Iraq after the 2003 United States invasion. It is unknown how many Iraqi civilians were wounded in the war: possibly as many were killed as were wounded.

The Watson Institute of International and Public Affairs at Brown University recommends that the US government should ensure that civilian deaths and injuries are included in public reporting of war deaths and should include a tally of children killed. As of 2018, the Watson Institute's findings are that over 182,000 civilians have died from direct war-related violence caused by the US, its allies, the Iraqi military and police, as well as opposition forces from the time of the invasion through November 2018. The violent deaths of Iraqi civilians have occurred through aerial bombing, shelling, gunshots, suicide attacks, and fires started by bombing.

Dr. Black learned through her patients that there were times when children were sent into the streets, hoping the drivers would refuse to hit a child and stop. But for the American drivers, if their trucks stopped, there were concerns that the vehicles would be ambushed or bombed.

The drivers reported they felt they had to keep driving, for the greater safety in the circumstance. Consequently, the children may have been run over.

"It was devastating to the Soldiers because most Soldiers did not join the military service to kill people. They joined to serve the country."

Another Soldier, when on a patrol, witnessed a group of civilians as they were hit by a mortar: "The explosion of blood just did this person in. I could feel the pain, I could visualize the image."

When spouses came in with Wounded Warriors, they often confided that the person they loved was no longer the person she or he was, both in manner and in physical ability. Dr. Black explains, "The loving anguish that the spouses carried was very moving." In fact, she has met many faithful marital couples, saying, "The capacity for love and acceptance is also very moving in and of itself; and yet, also very real was their anguish, grief, and anger, because their lives were going to be different. Forever." Some of the Soldiers, wondering if they could live with the grief they carried, would lay bare: "You know, I just don't think I can stay alive with this."

Per professional ethical guidelines, psychiatrists are not allowed to touch patients or do anything that would be considered disrespectful. What could be done was to help them continue their narratives, seek the appropriate care, and work to reconcile their faith, ethics, and orders of the military Mission in therapy.

Sometimes, after an appointment, Dr. Black would close the door and cry.

What was hoped from their encounter, other than some compensation, "was dropping their center of gravity; maybe dropping the hyper-arousal and the hyper-vigilance, and all those things that are characteristic, especially of combat PTSD, or experienced by people who have been around violence.

Maybe identifying a speck of an internal place that offers some centering or stability."

## Violence, trauma, grief, centering, acceptance, compassion as action

For Dr. Black, a practicing Buddhist and student of the Tibetan language with a religion degree, Psychiatry was the most compatible choice of medical specialty. Although Dr. Black started lecturing on Tibetan Medicine and Buddhist thought in her first year of medical school, it was never as a practitioner of Buddhist thought or Tibetan Medicine. "I always let the audience know I would never see a patient and say, 'So would you like to talk about Tibetan Buddhism?' That's completely unethical. But, when I lectured, I would speak about how this background helps me as a clinician."

She remembers someone saying—years ago, during her travels to northern India—that children represent the hope for the future.

"Now," Dr. Black says, "children everywhere are wondering if they have that hope for the future. A phrase that comes up a lot is, 'Well, I can't control anything.'

"We can always influence," observes Dr. Black, "from moment to moment; we influence everything right around us." The word, *influence*, she now substitutes for 'control,' particularly in therapeutic work but also in everyday parlance. One stance is that as a clinician, it is important to have the internal capacity to allow room for all the emotions people manifest, without taking them on; instead, the clinician should be able to acknowledge those emotions. Is this a compassionate act or stance?

## *"From moment to moment, we influence everything right around us."*

This is intended as an example of how compassion is not just something to talk about but is an activity to practice in our lives, in our day jobs, in our hearts. "This is how a person can maintain an inner-most self," Dr. Black demonstrates. "Compassion is more than that energy that goes outward but also having compassion for oneself. Compassion is bigger than empathy. Empathy implies that you've had an experience similar to mine, like 'I'll share your pain.' But compassion is bigger." It is a form of acceptance, as she understands fundamental Buddhist teachings, because of "the interdependent origination of all beings. It's the recognition that we're all in this together."

Compassion helps with the persistent 'stuckness' of grief and fear.

One prominent example of this, Dr. Black indicates, is that "the trauma of the legacy of slavery remains. It is not gone. The African American population feel this every day. They feel it inside their homes, they feel it on the streets because they still feel hunted, excluded. And inside the home, the multi-generational legacy, similar to that of Holocaust survivors, is an ongoing transmission of trauma."

The scary part of coming to terms with trauma is acceptance.

"Acceptance means a lot." Dr. Black's hope is that the external acceptance of others creates an internal acceptance of self, which allows for a bit of a shift, as opposed to internal blame, or self-hate. "What you are going to do for yourself is an internal shift, not just a behavioral shift. Most spiritual traditions teach a version of focusing outward, yes, on others, in the service of a higher consciousness in some form, which then helps you 'get over being locked in yourself.' This can be healing."

Influenced by the Buddhist practice, certain turns of phrase have been re-framed, when approaching and helping others heal from trauma. Dr. Black avoids using the words 'spiritual' and 'spiritual healing' because, on an emotional level, she observes many people feel protective of having their spirituality or religion taken from them, or fear that "you want them to be something else."

Instead, when she asks a patient *"what's closest to your heart?"* the reply may be 'my puppy' or 'my grandma.' "That phrase seems to be more neutral but still conveys a sense of something meaningful other than self." In the state of grief (or fear, or persistent traumatic symptoms) she says that *from moment to moment,* people can still be *'from the heart.'*

## Find Freedom—
## From centering to traveling
## outward and returning within

"There is a shift in the center of gravity when people pray," a word used to keep the metaphor for all the concomitant shifts Dr. Black mentioned. "It allows you to come more from the heart. Even if momentarily."

"But chronic lack of self-esteem rattles around in a lot of people; they don't really think of themselves as worthy," says the Rev. Eva Suarez, who believes that a part of the 'stuckness' we are feeling is that we aren't giving ourselves the chance to really nurse the thing that's wrong and then move through it. "They think if they work hard enough, they can prove that they're worthy." And, she points out, there's an obsession with status, "as if you should be able to tell the kind of person I am by looking at me. There's all this kind of judgment."

She likens how people prop themselves up—a measuring-stick for self-worth—to a portrayal of a golfer "who calls bad shots on a bad day and thinks of them as anomalies." This comes from a passage from the 1940 book, *The Problem of Pain*, by British writer and lay theologian C. S. Lewis (1898-1963). Rev. Suarez surmises that "he sees his greatest days of play as his real level, thinking *'that's who I really am.'*"

*We can't change what happened in the past, but we can make a better future by first reconciling ourselves with our past.*

Being new to hearing confession, Rev. Suarez reveals that people will "be feeling awful and sorry, but they won't actually be feeling sorry about the thing that they did wrong that they need to reconcile for. They'll be feeling shame about all this other stuff, about their own desires and their insecurity. You have to dig into why you did what you did. We need to move aside a lot of this shame."

Rev. Suarez, ordained to the priesthood in 2017 at the Washington National Cathedral, is indigenous to Washington, DC. Of her Brooklyn-born parents, her father's family came from Puerto Rico and her Jewish mother's, from the former USSR. It's quite a paradox, she says, that Christian spirituality, "remains powerful and life-giving in Latin America, despite it coming to the people through the worst of colonial brutality." Her Puerto Rican family lived through a fundamentally unjust system of colonial oppression. There is a lot she would change about the unjust policies "breaking the back of Puerto Rico today." We can't change what happened in the past, but we can make a better future by first reconciling ourselves with our past.

While she recognizes that "we can't un-ring bells and can't undo what's done," if she could go back and rewrite history, she would prevent the painful atrocities and slaughter of the Taino people—now an 'extinct' indigenous people of the Caribbean, and the natives of Puerto Rico.

> *"We can't un-ring bells*
> *and can't undo what's done."*

Yet, she says, the language of Christian spirituality is powerful and evocative for people all over Latin America. "Part of it is trusting God enough, that God loves us enough, and is in relationship with us enough that the terrible things we do to each other are not the whole story."

"We think something is so wrong with us," she says, and then reminds us again that this may not exactly true: "We're not getting at the heart of the need, which is a need to be loved and respected and cherished and to see ourselves as worthy of receiving love."

It's challenging for Rev. Suarez to talk with couples of any age, for instance, about sex and sexuality. "Because right now, that's all working well. That's part of why they're getting married. Right? They love each other. They're having a vigorous and healthy sex life." At the same time, she realizes how few people in their relationships are having real conversations about what they like and don't like. "With sexuality, people get confused about sex being wrong because we have this really puritanical culture. We get confused," Rev. Suarez says, as she contemplates the kinds of explorations that take place in premarital counseling. "How do you talk to them about how they speak with each other about what they like and don't like, and compromise with one another. Like when things change?"

Remember that when Barbara Streisand bats her eyelashes and says, "Love means never having to say you're sorry" in the 1972 screwball comedy *What's Up Doc?*, Ryan O'Neil's character responds in a deadpan voice, "That's the dumbest thing I ever heard." The apologetic cliché "Love means never having to say you're sorry"—the catchphrase spoken twice in the 1970 film *Love Story*?

"Bullshit," Rev. Suarez laughs.

"Love is challenging and difficult. Love is rigorous. It calls on a lot of us. It is different than just feeling good or just feeling at peace or just enjoying. We say this word 'love' and put it in a box on Valentine's Day. That's too easy. Or, you just say it every day, not thinking about it, not intending to say this big thing. When everybody's loving something—'loving my car, loving my wife, loving the house, loving my children, loving the earth'—I don't feel that they mean that all in the same way. That's lip service. There's no action behind it."

The awakening we want is blocked by confusion. Rev. Suarez observes, "People can't tease out the difference between what they like, their values, and what feels good. 'If we're feeling good, things must be good.'"

## Coming Out As Worthy

This chapter is the beginning of a progression in which is it very important to be quiet, to not do very much yet except to listen. In centering, our traumas can start to soften. The old self becomes quieted, and the worthy self will emerge. Coming out as being worthy of love is an essential step toward freedom. I want you to see me, well and good, but not with a kinship of common suffering.

> *Coming out as being worthy of love is an essential step towards freedom.*

Coming out as worthy in the broadest sense of the word—worthy of love and living on the planet—is not a one-time thing. I am always coming out in new ways.

Coming out, on behalf of others, restores dignity to our all being here. You have to be the first to give freely. I extrapolate the universal notion of 'coming out' as showing up for all the important causes that should be spoken up for. It might be to put a stop to bullying, domestic violence, or a coworker who robs others of fairness; or to start anew.

But the narrowest definition of coming out—yes, the one reserved specifically for saying to others that our sexual identity and self-expression is different than what it 'should be' according to the standards of society—isn't something we do alone.

As it turns out, people's appetite for fearlessness has come a long way. And 2016 was an especially good year for coming out.

Queen Elizabeth's cousin Lord Ivar Mountbatten became the first member of the extended Royal family to reveal he is gay. Speaking to the *Daily Mail* in 2016, the fifty-three-year-old said, "Being a Mountbatten was never the problem; it was the generation into which I was born. When I was growing up, it was known as 'the love that dare not speak its name,' but what's amazing now is how far we have all come in terms of acceptance."

"'Coming out' is such a funny phrase," he humors the labeling, "but it's what I suppose I did in a rather roundabout way, emerging to a place I'm happy to be. I have struggled with my sexuality and in some ways I still do; it has been a real journey to reach this point. I was driven into the closet by not wanting to come to terms with who I was and facing friends and family in the early years. I buried it. I'm just so pleased now to have found someone who I am happy to call my partner."

Well into my late forties, a lack of self-worth persisted. It rose to the surface as I began seeing, and sharing with my mother, national news stories about Mike Pence advocating for gay conversion therapy. In July 2016, Mr. Pence was forefront in national headlines as a Vice Presidential candidate.

Conversion therapy, a controversial practice that seeks to change a person's sexual orientation from gay to straight, is banned in only five states including California, Oregon, Illinois, Vermont and New Jersey. Given Mr. Pence's strong and extensive opposition to LGBTQ rights, his words have been widely interpreted as supporting the controversial practice. Pence again angered gay rights groups in 2015 when he signed a religious freedom bill that opponents said would allow businesses to discriminate against customers based on their sexual orientation. Mr. Pence later backtracked when state lawmakers changed the law to say that "no discrimination would be allowed."

One day, an apology came. Not from Mike Pence, but from my mother. Not wanting to go to her grave inadvertently having done such a wrong, she said that no person should be subject to being forced to not be who they are; no person should be forced to hide, nor to even stay hidden by choice; to be persecuted, nor hate what you are supposed to be naturally; and, most importantly, no person should not be loved.

She did not make excuses. It was different than an amends or restitution; not really a textbook apology. This time, she took personal responsibility for her relationship with her own ideas; it gave her freedom.

*This time, she took personal responsibility for her relationship with her own ideas; it gave her freedom.*

As I listened, I accepted the apology with an awareness that this was not for me, but for the many, many tens of millions of people, in all times and places in history, who would so truly love such a sincere offering of regret, acceptance, and self-possession from their parent. She evoked compassion for people who choose to stay closeted. I accepted the level of true sincerity with which she spoke about how nothing matters more to how we should act than our own self-worth. Most people who are judged wrongly, just for being who they are or want to be, will never receive this apology. When a healing is given — all sides receive it.

This event was a Big Goodbye. It feels good to write things off, to control the balance sheet, to keep the temple clean.

*When a healing is given — all sides receive it.*

As Dr. Black says to people all the time and has a 'note to self' in the office: *Always wear joy and always be ready for something wonderful to happen.*

Most important is living the prayer.

The word 'prayer' as a generic term, says Dr. Black, "can be used as 'a centering, a quieting,' and for a shift of the focus, from moment to moment, to something greater. And most often, for a sense of a purpose: something that has meaning greater than oneself."

Her prayer has three verbs: Feel, Live, and Be.

# Prayer

*for*
*Worthy of Love*

# "Be Peace, Feel Peace, Breathe Peace, Live Peace"

By Nancy B. Black, MD, Colonel, US Army, Retired

*Be Peace.*
*Feel Peace.*
*Breathe Peace.*
*Live Peace.*

*Like for the Soldiers and their Families, for
all to whom a legacy of healing is offered,
we each have a personal responsibility—the
ability, to create a version of acceptance
in the world, externally, that will move us
toward an acceptance in ourselves.*

*To arrive and be there, you can also:*

*Feel heart.*
*Live heart.*
*Be heart.*

# Freedom
# to Share

Lawren Harris (1885-1970). *Lake Superior*, 1923. Oil on canvas.
The Thomson Collection at the Art Gallery of Ontario, Toronto.

*"O Hidden Life, vibrant in every atom;*
*O Hidden Light, shining in every creature;*
*O Hidden Love, embracing all in Oneness;*
*May all who feel themselves as one with Thee,*
*Know they are therefore one with every other."*

These lines have been set to music. They have been
chanted and sung. Written in 1923 by Dr. Annie Besant, an
English philosopher, women's rights activist, and prolific
author regarded as a champion of human freedom, many
meanings may be discovered to transform our world.
"When we repeat these few simple lines, either alone or in
a group," reckons Joy Mills, President of the Theosophical
Society of America from 1965-1974, "We invoke the One
Reality to manifest itself anew, and this is to make whole
and make holy all that is in the universe about us. No more
wonderful act could we perform."

## Healing with Others

External acceptance and moments of peace, Dr. Nancy Black showed, can help heal from the outside in.

As we progress, we join in healing with others. As you become more worthy of love, you leave the realm of inner aloneness; joining others in their aspiration, freedom returns straight to center stage. But the paradox in taking personal responsibility for freedom is to clearly remember that outer circumstances are not how we find self-worth. Groups or organizations, or even our ancestral traditions, are not of any true significance unless they help us to claim freedom together. Getting out of hell, we have said over and over, is breaking free from freedom that has been corrupted. Now it is time to learn that freedom is constructed out of the ways in which we share our inner selves.

*Now it is time to learn that freedom is constructed out of the ways in which we share our inner selves.*

Remarkably, two women who will never meet in real life—coming from entirely different times in history, countries, ancestries and faith traditions—have something vigorously similar to say about this.

Rev. Eva Suarez says, in scripture as in life, "To get to the settled place, we have to be allowed to dig into the parts that are in our heart."

Blanche Rachel Mirra Alfassa (born 1878 in Paris and died 1973 in India), known to her followers as 'The Mother' taught that "genuine sincerity is the only thing that is needed to elevate you. Through it, we get an unfailing courage." Originally written in French, her *Prayers and Meditations* have been translated into English, allowing more people to hear her guidance that "all obstacles can be surmounted."

The Mother underpins that people still may think their condition depends on external circumstances. But this is all false, she affirms. "If somebody is a 'nervous wreck,' he thinks if circumstances are favourable he will improve. But, actually, even if they are favourable, he will remain what he is. All think they are feeling weak and tired because people are not nice to them. This is rubbish. It is not the circumstances that have to be changed: what is required is an inner change. If you feel that a change is needed, it can be in the attitude, giving importance to what is to be said and realised and using the past as a preparation for the future. This is not a very difficult thing to do—and I am quite sure that you will easily do it."

Nor are meditation and prayer impractical. They help people transcend their worries, pain, and scars, the spiritual degeneracy that leads to compulsions.

A woman who uses farming as a mediation says, "There is no difference between meditation and ordinary activities." Her taking care of the land is meditation enough because it is compassionate. There is less worry because there is action; there is less compulsion because there is effort; there is less fear because there is experience, observation, and knowing.

For such a quieting technique, The Mother can fuel you with the kind of firm gusto you may be needing...

"But where to get such a strength? Within you. The Divine Presence is in you. It is in you. You look for it outside; look inside. It is in you. The Presence is there. You want the appreciation of others to get strength—you will never get it. The strength is in you. If you want, you can aspire for what seems to you the supreme goal, supreme light, supreme knowledge, supreme love. But it is in you—otherwise, you would never be able to contact it. If you go deep enough inside you, you will find it there, like a flame that is always burning straight up.

And don't believe that it is difficult to do. It is because the look is always turned outside that you don't feel the Presence. But if, instead of looking outside for support, you concentrate and you pray—inside, to the supreme knowledge—to know at each moment what is to be done, the way to do it, and if you give all you are, all you do in order to acquire perfection, you will feel that the support is always there, always guiding, showing the way. And if there is a difficulty, then instead of wanting to fight, you hand it over, hand it over to the supreme wisdom to deal with it—to deal with all the bad wills, all the misunderstandings, all the bad reactions. If you surrender completely, it is no more your concern: it's the concern of the Supreme who takes it up and knows better than anybody else what is to be done. That is the only way out, only way out. There, my child."

The Mother nicely compliments the conditions for this depth of sincerity. She observes that "freedom does not come from outer circumstances but from inner liberation. Don't fail to remember," she writes, "that satisfaction does not depend on outer circumstances but on an inner condition."

Healing our inner condition to find some measure of inner liberation may begin as a solo one, but it is how we *share* our inner liberation with each other that counts in the aspiration to freedom.

> *...It is how we share our inner liberation with each other that counts in the aspiration to freedom.*

As we move from thinking about ourselves to healing with others, there is a healing advantage of sitting quietly with other people—in a group, instead of solo. Group prayers help the feelings of aloneness we often experience in life. Don't get isolated; participate in life, in communities where service, group activities, movement, and meditation raise people's spirits. When we are gathered with others, it helps us to listen and to silence the mental chatter, that every-day phenomena Buddhists call the restless and confused 'monkey mind.'

Back in our school days, we found a happiness by walking around together in a pack. I still experience it and recall the heart-centered words in the prologue to the book *Boys in the Boat*. The author notes that when the surviving members of the crew occasionally reunite, "There is nothing better than being together." My school headmaster, Benjamin Williams of Cate School, has also noticed that when alumni gather, it isn't necessarily to talk or socialize. "Oftentimes," he says, "they just want to be in each other's presence. There is something to be said for that, surely."

The healing actions taken in groups build strength. Most important is transforming our inner strength into action, to have the maturity to take our fidelity, fearlessness, and honesty out into the world.

From listening to other people, you provide service; as you advance, it is seeing with the eye of the heart. With a hearty chuckle, Rev. Suarez admits that she sometimes needs to actually be able to talk out loud. "I put myself in that category of people who can sometimes struggle to be quiet, and rest in it." Where there is a lot of silence and contemplation, centering prayer is sort of a challenge: "to be in the presence of God while in the presence of others. There's something powerful about a group of people all coming to look for the same thing in the same place, or to look for different things in the same place; a group investment in a place with group love."

## Group Love: Ways People Come Together

Entering group love of any kind is not unlike your first day in elementary school where you simply have no choice but to dive in. It's fun to congregate. Even if you're grieving.

Let's do dinner, shall we?

'The Dinner Party' and 'The People's Supper' are building a worldwide community of sharing meals. The Dinner Party is for people in their twenties and thirties, all of whom have lost someone significant in their lives. Founded by Carla Fernandez and Lennon Flowers, it is a dinner party where "you keep coming back and realize your heartache can also help create amazing friendships and forward motion in your life."

The family dinner table is 'sacred ground' in the Fernandez family, so when Carla Fernandez's dad passed away from brain cancer, coming back to the table was "a natural way for Carla to connect with others and unpack the experience of life after loss."

Joining the club nobody wants to join, "You feel a little bit like an alien." You find out about the dinner party, are matched to a table...and you go.

The Dinner Party sets tables for people who have 'first-dinner nerves.' "Bring what you can—a bottle of wine or a loaf of bread—ring the doorbell or text your host and find yourself in a room with other people around your age who have also experienced significant loss." Once everyone grabs something to eat, the host will start the conversation and "You'll introduce yourself and share what brings you to the table and where you are with your loss right now. The conversation will flow, and you'll listen while others do the same."

The Dinner Party's co-founder Lennon Flowers lost her mother during her senior year of college, following a four-year fight with lung cancer. "Three years later, she hitched up her wagon and headed West," 3,000 miles away from home. She found she no longer had anyone with whom she could talk about her mom and explore the way in which her life, death, and absence continued to affect her. When Carla, a friend, colleague, and soon-to-be roommate, invited her over for dinner, it was a 'no-brainer.'

In January 2017, together with partners at Faith Matters Network and Hollaback!, Flowers launched The People's Supper: a nationwide effort "to create healing spaces that strengthen our individual and collective resilience and wellbeing and to repair the breach in our interpersonal relationships across political, ideological, and identity differences."

The participants of the People's Supper heal internally through actively meeting with and supporting others; they seek to build the foundations of their new, post-grief selves out of shared experiences and compassion.

## A Rigor to Life in Balance

Rev. Suarez's take is different, helping us see that sometimes it's not even about a 'whole new foundation' as much as it is getting rid of the stuff that doesn't work for us anymore.

In social work, she learned about ego defenses, skills that we develop to protect ourselves, but which stop working after a while: "They become overdeveloped, and then become part of harming ourselves — like denial. There's actually a lot of good stuff about denial." She observes how denial helps us accept information at a pace that we can actually absorb it without being overwhelmed by it but warns that "if we cling too much to denial, it becomes the whole story, and rewrites the truth."

*"If we cling too much to denial, it becomes the whole story, and rewrites the truth."*

And to her, that feels a lot like what's happening with our climate crisis.

Just like the environment, we are ecosystems ourselves, where parts need to be happening in proportion with each other.

Inside myself, I have learned a constructive way to build a stronger team, recognizing that egos are there to protect us.

Yet, egos are unbearably loud, and when my ego is angry, I need to become the officiating umpire of a baseball team telling it to *'play well with the others.'* You mustn't wound it. Wounded egos scream at our minds and hearts: *why is this happening to me?* Simply letting the ego know that it is not in charge of all the other players helps tame it. If it can't stop behaving like a misfit child, if it insists on having its way, it needs to be told to *'sit this game out.'* Whatever is happening, don't scream back at it. When it is fuming safely on the bench, the other parts of ourselves can be heard and listened to. Thereby we build a stronger team.

We should be permeable internally, allowing emotions to pass through and be released. When we apply attention to building stronger internal ecosystems, our responses to the external environment we live in becomes stronger and more balanced.

People really struggle, Rev. Suarez believes, because they want the natural world to be strong and impervious to us: "We want to think of the world as going on and on forever, every resource as being able to withstand us. We might say "elephants are so big and strong: why do I have to protect an elephant?" That same vulnerability—that reliance on one another that we often despair of in ourselves or reject—is what we're ignoring in the environment: that we have to take care of one another, and we need to be cared for."

We all have much to learn about Thanksgiving, and its three fundamental principles of gratitude, mourning, and joy. For what is our healing now, if not from climate grief?

For native peoples, Thanksgiving comes not once a year, but always, for all the gifts of life. All native nations have celebrations of the harvest that come from very ancient traditions. Although it is the anniversary of a beginning for the white man in America, some people also recall the untold story connected with Thanksgiving, remembering that for native peoples, the original Americans, it is a day of mourning for being silenced, enslaved, overtaken through theft of land and culture, with intentional and unintentional discrimination.

Now 350 years later, native peoples are re-envisioning a new beginning for themselves. Their collective identity, as people "living on this land that at this time is called the

United States of America," Thanksgiving can grow into an all-inclusive ceremony.

It is just as Rev. Brenda Husson welcomed us to see in the 'Prayers' chapter: "We are invited into the holy feast of love… we are meant to join in and complete that circle."

> *"We are invited into the holy feast of love…we are meant to join in and complete that circle."*

In northeast North America, the 'Six Nations' known as the Iroquois Confederacy employ a group prayer of thanksgiving said at the beginning and end of meetings, social events, ceremonies, and whenever people are gathered together. "We can also say it as a morning and evening prayer," declares Brad Bonaparte of the Mohawk Nation territory. "When we say this prayer, we can change it according to how we feel at the moment."

Sometimes thanks are given for all of the cosmos, and sometimes thanks are given individually to the elements of the world. "Most of the time, the prayer is somewhere in the middle, just as long as all creation is included. Every day we are alive, even if we are not feeling well or we're in a bad mood or we have a flat tire, we give thanks to all the elements of Creation. We take comfort in knowing that, when we pass on, these things will continue." Through the thanksgiving ceremony, each person reads, with a bell sounded after each paragraph.

Honoring all our ancestors, we deepen our connection with the past. Learning about and understanding the current situation, we deepen our connection with the present. Co-creating a newly integrative and inclusive vision, we deepen our connection with the future. Thanksgiving comes not once a year for native peoples "but always, for all the gifts of life."

# Prayer

*for*
*Freedom to Share*

# "Thanksgiving Address of the Kaianerekowa Hotinonsionne/ The Great Law of Peace"

By the Iroquois/Haudenosaunee Confederacy

Address:

I ask everyone to bring their minds together as one and to give thanks and acknowledgment of the Creator for Mother Earth that she continue to support all life forms. (bell)

As we look around the Creation, we see different things. We see the waters. We acknowledge their gift to us, from the smallest streams to the largest rivers to the oceans. We give thanks to them that they continue with their duties of refreshing us and cleansing us and bringing life. We bring all our minds together as one and give thanks. (bell)

Now we turn our minds to the plants that grow upon the Earth, from the smallest grasses, to the berries, to the fruit plants to the medicine plants, to the Three Sisters—corn, beans, and squash—and up to the trees, to the head of all the plants,

to the maple trees. We give thanks to
them that they continue with their duties
of providing us with food, shelter, and
beauty. We bring all our minds together
as one and give thanks. (bell)

Now we turn our minds to all the
creatures who walk or crawl on the
Earth. We give thanks to them that they
continue with their duties of providing
us with food, clothing, and beauty. We
bring all our minds together as one and
give thanks. (bell)

Now we turn our minds to all the creatures
who live in the water. We give thanks to
them that they continue with their duties of
keeping the water fresh and clean, and providing us with food. We bring all our minds
together as one and give thanks. (bell)

Now we turn our minds to all the creatures who fly in the sky. We give thanks
to them that they continue with their

duties of providing us with food, songs, and beauty. We bring all our minds together as one and give thanks. (bell)

Now as we go higher in the sky, we turn our minds to our Grandfathers the Thunders. We give thanks to them that they continue with their duties of bringing the rains that will help our gardens. We bring all our minds together as one and give thanks. (bell)

Now we turn our minds to the Wind. We give thanks to the wind, that the wind continues with the duty of bringing clean air for us to breathe. We bring all our minds together as one and give thanks. (bell)

Now we turn our minds to the Four Skydwellers. We give thanks to you that you continue with your duties of giving us our instructions on how we treat one another and the world around us. We bring all our minds together as one and give thanks. (bell)

Now we turn our minds to our Grandmother Moon. We give thanks to you that you continue with your duties of controlling the life cycles of the women, so that the Earth will continue in its cycle of life. We bring all our minds together as one and give thanks. (bell)

Now we turn our minds to our Brother Sun. We give thanks to you that you continue with your duties of providing us with light and warmth to help our plants to grow. We bring all our minds together as one and give thanks. (bell)

Now we turn our minds to our Cousins the Stars. We give thanks to you that you continue with your duties of providing beauty and light in the nighttime sky. We bring all our minds together as one and give thanks. (bell)

Now we turn our minds to Handsome Lake. We give thanks to you for reminding our people of their original instructions on how to work with one another and how to give thanks. We bring all our minds together as one and give thanks. (bell)

Now we turn our minds to the Creator. We give thanks to the creator for providing all these different things that will help and sustain our lives. We bring all our minds together as one and give thanks. (bell)

Now we return to the Earth, and we look at all the people who are gathered here and we give thanks that we have all come together with good thoughts and good minds, to share and learn from one another. We bring all our minds together as one and give thanks. (bell)

# Making Friends

Winslow Homer (1836-1910). *Nuit d'été*
(Summer Night), 1890. Oil on canvas.

Musée d'Orsay, Paris.

*"Life's magic is always
right here in front of us."*

—Tom Vendetti,
filmmaker

"When you went to camp for two weeks—two whole weeks!—I really missed you for the first twenty-four hours." My mother savored that rare fragrance of deliverance from the daily binds of motherhood. Those 'return to nature' summers intended to help me be a healthy boy.

The YMCA packed us up, colorful and bright eight-to-ten-year-olds, with ample survival gear and food to keep us warm and alive for two weeks. Some of the nicest young adults imaginable guided us, spiritually as well as physically. We were shown the peaceful road. Steering into Yellowstone National Park in Wyoming, the lot of us, the youngest outbackers in the West were implanted within the dramatic canyons, alpine rivers, lush forests, hot springs, and gushing geysers, including the most famous one of all, Old Faithful.

Visits to Nature are a high contrast to the social Darwinism of schoolrooms and workplaces, and streets ('*beware of becoming an outcast, be on guard, don't be vulnerable, be like your heroes, don't be too weird, save that for when people already know you a little bit*'). We opened our throats in a choir of anti-war protest songs "If I Had a Hammer" and "Peace Train," and slept not inside tents or cabins, but under tarps, the night stars above the great sand dunes inculcating in us a fearless endurance to see how strong we really were.

We carried our own provisions, gas stoves, and water. I hated everything about it. I hated being dirty. I hated my friends being dirty. I hated the insects. I hated heights. The only thing I liked was the arts, where we got to sing around the campfire and make things.

Nature was horrible.

When we want to make life less vulgar, we look instead to beautify it. But over time, my desire for the protective shield of elegance fused with what Nature offers: a friend. We learned to be friends. Nature is more often seen as a mother, but the one who doesn't judge our looks, our shape, our charm. Form a friendship with the Sequoia forests and you will have more than a cathedral of trees whom the National Park Service rangers serve and protect. You will know again how to make friends wherever you go.

*But over time, my desire for the protective shield of elegance fused with what Nature offers: a friend. We learned to be friends.*

Now, tell me why we carry on having a pervasive illusion of separation from Nature.

In the slim 192-page paperback, *I Seem to Be A Verb*, inventor Buckminster Fuller asserts a declaration of freedom from how we see ourselves as human beings: we are not things to be controlled.

Fuller's assertion that "I know that I am not a category" defies even the biggest categorizations, like those in our birth certificates, which says I am human, a boy, a girl, a genetically encoded Homo sapien.

Instead, he reveals, "I seem to be a verb, an evolutionary process—an integral function of the universe."

This indicates seeing no separation between the environment and man's future. "The matter changes when we deeply realize," he says, "that the nature 'out there' and the nature 'in here' are one and the same, that the sense of separation—no matter how pervasive—is nonetheless totally illusory." He would call the need for such realization "the central psychological or spiritual challenge of our age."

This lack of distance (lack of separation) is also newly evident between native peoples and the rest of the world. It reinforces why many feel that *indigenous spirituality is not a luxury but a necessity.*

That is because externally-focused change—all the things we try to do in society to create happiness in the external world (partnership, business, human progress, relationships, coming out)—can seem a hard proposition, about which there is much bitterness. Dignity and freedom are aspirational and difficult to gain (or regain).

We are told that "everyone has the right to respect and dignity" by United Nations Secretary-General Ban Ki-moon in his message on World Mental Health Day. "Everyone is entitled to their hopes and dreams—to work, enjoy family and friends, go about their life without stigma and discrimination, and participate in decisions that affect them."

We hear and demand all the time that 'things have to change' and 'I have to change' but it's no good if you don't know how. Unfortunately, a cynical-leaning truism is that people don't change much, because they don't like to change, especially when the money faucets are rolling; we get cynical and cozy with ugliness but not immune to it; we change only when we absolutely must. When the pressure is on, we easily come right back to square one: feelings of obligation to 'fix' our stressed world, without getting to the causes of our grief.

However, we can both see and do this differently. Change comes with desired and positive effects when we educate about and re-learn how to make friends. Only you can change yourself, says Emmy-award winning documentary filmmaker Tom Vendetti, but he also had to find out for himself how to do it. Culturally, not just from traveling and documenting, nor from just helping others as a psychologist, but ultimately by going into his own heart.

What he has discovered aligns with a powerful vision of native peoples who also do not see separation between man and the environment. Shining a light on the separation reveals we do not need to put up walls, even when we are angry, and despite a serious impasse about Nature that has existed for a very long time between European languages of the West, the Far East, and First Nations. It is this impasse we can see differently as we move together toward freedom.

A metamorphic transformation occurred for Tom Vendetti when, at fifty-five, he found out that 99 percent of his prostate had cancer. "It was like being hit in the head with a two-by-four, a wakeup call," as he went and had the radioactive seeds—122 of them—put in his prostate. Depressed, lying in bed, he said to his wife: "I need to go to Nepal." He felt weak, but he kept saying he needed to go there.

"I love mountains...I want to go to the mountains," Tom kept calling out.

"Then you should go," his wife said, speaking to his calling.

Until the cancer, Tom was not the kind of person to believe in anything to do with being guided by synchronicity, divine timing, or magic. Here was a psychologist with an optimistic personality. Getting his PhD, doing a dissertation, "everything had to be objective," even when he worked with the mentally ill, many of whom were psychotic. His psychologist's trade was always empirical.

Yet, as he got up into the high mountains of the Himalayas, things that were "almost magical" started happening. Chance meetings with the very people who had ascended and filmed *Everest*, each a signal of fate, at precise moments, would be pivotal. As if tailor-made, "it was that quiet time again, being able to hike and be in Nature" that brought him back to life. He calls this a 'feel good' challenge, one we can all take, because "beauty is a very important part of the exposure that people need."

Before his healing from cancer in the mountains, Tom played a small game with himself. He got up one day and went to work thinking he was going to count the number of negative thoughts that came into his head—for just one day—to see how prevalent they were. By ten or eleven o'clock in the morning, there were so many, he had to stop counting. That was a huge wake-up call. He had no idea he was thinking all these negative thoughts on such a regular basis. "Number one, becoming aware of it, made me conscious that I can change this. I'm in self-imposed suffering; I'm doing this to myself. And it really doesn't have to happen. If you're aware of it, and you want to change it, you can."

> ## "If you're aware of it, and you want to change it, you can."

He called his wife from the mountains, and she detected something new was occurring in him. She said, "I've never heard you sound so happy." He felt a true sense of inner peace, true happiness. Contemplating the meaning behind all the wonderful experiences, the mountains kept calling him. They have taught him that "life's magic is always right here in front of us." Out of this experience, he made *When the Mountain Calls,* a film reflecting on his thirty years of travels in Nepal. How he anchors to taking action, he says, is that when he finds himself helping others, it makes him feel good.

"You're either going to be in despair, or you're going to be in integrity," and he wants to look back in his life, be in integrity and feel like he's had an impact. That usually means doing something positive for other communities or society.* "That's where I'm coming from, in terms of my final days here on this planet."

You can also take making friends from the personal to the professional, informs Jessica Rockwood, another agent of change. "Malaria Zero," "Roll Back Malaria," and "Global Fund to Fight AIDS" roll off her lips, as if saving lives is a fluency all its own.

Halting infectious diseases, and eliminating malaria is a huge task, from Zimbabwe, Sierra Leone, Ethiopia, Nigeria, Ghana, Namibia, and Kenya in Africa to Hispaniola in the Amazon or in Asia Pacific. On any given day, you would stand a very good chance of finding Jessica, President of International Public Health Advisors, en route to any of these nations.

---

*  *A gentle footstep for Tom Vendetti, in the realm of cross-cultural music, has touched the lives of forty orphan and underprivileged children in Cambodia who were taught how to play the ukulele in tandem with native Hawaiian musicians. The musicians and the children are conscious of preserving their ancient language and traditional music, while bringing happiness.*

*Recorded in Nepal, Tibet, and Bhutan, Vendetti's concept album Himalayan Sessions benefits the Aloha Music Camp, in tandem with native Hawaiian musicians who blend music that reflects the ancient mountain lands. He compiled the songs recorded for his documentaries Journey Inside Tibet, Mount Kailash: return to Tibet, Tibetan Illusion Destroyer, and When the Mountain Calls - Nepal, Tibet & Bhutan. It combines the music of composer Paul Horn (1930-2014), an American flutist and pioneer of world music, with interviews Vendetti conducted with the Dalai Lama in Kathmandu, India.*

Zambia is another story. "I've never seen more hope," Rockwood beams. "The people on the ground at the community level are the most inspirational people I've met. It is absolutely about relationships," she confirms resoundingly. "They've got malaria rates down so low, through real engagement at the community level and at the cross-border levels, that in southern Zambia, we could actually see almost total elimination of malaria. The country wants to do it by 2021; but by 2023, in regions of Zambia, you will see the elimination of malaria, which is incredibly inspiring. They are really a shining moment in the world of malaria."

Through relationships, she says, we come to understand how doable something is. 'Small interventions' at a community, country, or district level, can leave an impact. Face-to-face community engagement is how we're going to move forward as a culture. "That intervention is good at the personal or community level, as well as the macro," and she fundamentally weighs that "it is a process that is between people."

*"Intervention is good at the personal or community level, as well as the macro—it is a process that is between people."*

They are only now starting to make it work, but Jessica sees beyond slow and steady progress with donors, policymakers, and religious leaders. The capacity for community-level change is about broadening these relationships.

Tom Vendetti, on the other hand, was initially extremely skeptical when he was invited by the government of Bhutan to make the first film about "gross national happiness."

He interviewed the Prime Minister about the four pillars of the government that promote happiness. First, a transparent and fair government that truly represents the people; second, an environment that is beautiful; third, for the country to have economic stability by providing free health care to everyone. The last pillar is preserving their culture—primarily a Buddhist culture—and preserving those values.

But he came to see, on a national level, a government actively promoting happiness for the people, as opposed to gross national productivity or "the capitalist type of approach that seems to stress a lot of people out." Interestingly, their investigations into what made people happy coincided with important environmental improvements. Before they started the concept, a percentage of the forest was being destroyed, whereas now, 80 percent or more of the forest is being preserved. "This could become a model for the world," he says, "because in general, the people did appear much happier."

Meanwhile, in democratic societies like America, this isn't yet happening. What we do is compete to win. America's dimming reputation as a 'beacon of freedom' may be obvious, but beacons of freedom are people, not societies. Our exploration of a new future is born inside ourselves.

To restore freedom, the moral question is not of 'compete first, make friends later.' It is not, as author Richard

A. Bowell writes, "To sacrifice other human lives as the price that is needed to be paid for a smaller and smaller 'select' (self-selected) group of us to continue." For until all life is sacred, Bowell has petitioned the United Nations to see, "No life can live in a sacred way here on this planet, and this all begins in a new value for human life inside ourselves."

The question, therefore, is how to make friends *while* competing to win. Is that concept so impossible? Not when we reflect on the formula we have traversed in this book's urge to find freedom. The story of the old Jews is about leaving 400 years of slavery after Pharaoh. The progression to freedom is the same now as then: 1) turn away from freedom corrupted (all that is manipulated, maneuvered, taken from us), 2) retrain ourselves, and 3) find freedom.

Why do you make a friend? Can you even remember? A real friend is not self-serving. A friend wants the best for you. This lighthearted aphorism jests: "Good friends offer advice and wisdom. Best friends come over unannounced with vodka, superhero costumes, glitter, fireworks, and bacon." I'm always on the lookout to make friends with ideas foreign to mine because I don't want any idea to be foreign.

The fork in the road is to either go on possessing, controlling, and problem-solving, which regards solutions as things, or to make advancements through things we don't possess, seeing ourselves as verbs: solution seekers, finders, pilgrims. The fulfilled life, the covenant of our essential humanity is always in relationship, not in competition, with others.

> *The fulfilled life, the covenant of our essential humanity is always in relationship, not in competition, with others.*

It's not healthy to be superior. Superiority becomes the colonial, political class of empire, and our ideological pride. Pride, in common parlance, is often thought to be a good thing, but as a famously deadly sin, it is devoid of love and essentially destructive. Don't be one of those people who brushes it off 'guilty as charged.'

That's not making friends.

Instead, as Fred Rogers used to say, "Look for the helpers. You will always find people who are helping."

Tom Vendetti discovered that while greater awareness leads to healing, if you really want to effect change on a societal basis, it's self-evident you can't do it through prayer and meditation alone. Ringing a bell, going to a concert, meditating—that's all well and good—but there has to be action, the Dalai Lama told Tom. The Dalai Lama isn't discounting prayer or meditation in terms of an individual practice, but to really change society, it must come through education and educating the population. The awareness for compassion and dignity, and the concepts of what they are about, starts at an early age.

Where it comes to making friends with Nature, I recommend Denmark's public education system that develops the factors that create empathy.

*Ringing a bell, going to a concert, meditating—that's all well and good— but there has to be action—and to really change society, it has to come through education and educating the population.*

## Compassion and prayer make human feelings expansive; our empathy does the same for the earth.

Teaching empathy, mandatory since 1993 in Denmark schools, is a factor that contributes to the happiness of the country. Lessons in empathy—preparing children to become happy adults—has three teachable components:

- Teamwork, in which 60 percent of the tasks at school are carried out, the focus is not to excel over others but to have a responsibility in helping those who are not equally gifted.

- Competition is exclusively with oneself, not with others. Danish schools offer neither prizes nor trophies to their students who excel in school subjects or in sports, so as not to create competition. Instead, they practice the culture of motivation to improve, measured exclusively in relation to themselves.

- Collaborative learning, which consists of bringing together children with different strengths and weaknesses in different subjects to make them help each other in class, working together on various projects. The latter method teaches children from an early age that one cannot succeed alone, and that helping others leads to better results.

A full hour—every week—in Danish schools is dedicated to the "Klassens tid," an empathy lesson for students aged six to sixteen years. A fundamental part of the Danish curriculum, "The hour of empathy is as important as the time spent, for example, on English or mathematics," reports *Morning Future* (the blog shaped by the Addeco Group in Italy).

During the Klassens tid, students discuss their problems, either related to school or not, and the whole class, together with the teacher, tries to find a solution based on real listening and understanding. "If there are no problems to discuss, children simply spend the time together relaxing and enjoying 'hygge,' a word (also a verb and an adjective), which cannot be translated literally, since it is a phenomenon closely related to Danish culture. 'Hygge' could be defined as 'intentionally created intimacy.'"

In Denmark, a country where it gets dark, rainy, and gray very early in the year, 'hygge' means bringing light, warmth, and friendship, creating a shared, welcoming and intimate atmosphere. It is a fundamental concept for the Danish sense of well-being. And it's also a global phenomenon: Amazon sells more than 900 books on 'hygge,' and Instagram has more than three million posts with the hashtag #hygge.

By becoming fluent in empathy, we can shake it up at work, in the gym, on the way to school, texting your next date, servicing clients, climbing a career ladder—until it is second nature in all we do.

Making friends has to be harder hitting. It requires action. We are lacking that action. Compassion is a word, but it means nothing if we do nothing.

Just as we need friends, we need Nature. We cannot be happy without Nature. Further, let's push our imaginations to see that the exact same empathy we can learn to give people can equally be given to water, trees, the earth's energy resources.

You may visit a beautiful place, by a lake or river or trek into the mountains, and yet, the effects are likely to be temporary, not lasting. To retain the good feeling and stabilize them, we need to release ourselves from the inability to see beauty in each other and in the world. When you are in the presence of something or someone you feel is enlightened, whether a great work of art, music, book, or person, you feel good.

For painter Georgia O'Keeffe (1887-1986), as she contemplated the art of seeing, she wrote, "To see takes time, like to have a friend takes time." She found she could "say things with color and shapes" that she couldn't say in any other way, things for which she had no words.

The artist emphatically denied interpretations that her depictions of flowers were a commentary on women's sexuality. In an exhibition catalog published in 1939 by An American Place, *Georgia O'Keeffe-exhibition of oils and pastels*, she writes:

"A flower is relatively small. Everyone has many associations with a flower—the idea of flowers. You put out your hand to touch the flower—lean forward to smell it—maybe touch it with your lips almost without thinking—or give it to someone to please them. Still—in a way—nobody sees a flower—really—it is so small—we haven't time—and to see takes time, like to have a friend takes time. If I could paint the flower exactly as I see it no one would see what I see because I would paint it small like the flower is small. So I said to myself—I'll paint what I see—what the flower is to me but I'll paint it big and they will be surprised into taking time to look at it—I will make even busy New Yorkers take time to see what I see of flowers. Well—I made you take time to look at what I saw and when you took time to really notice my flower, you hung all your own associations with flowers on my flower and you write about my flower as if I think and see what you think and see of the flower—and I don't."

American essayist Maria Popova, whose love of great thinkers includes O'Keeffe, has written that the flowers were O'Keeffe's commentary on seeing: "A magnifying lens for the attention. Painting these close-ups was a way of learning to look, a way of removing the blinders with which we gallop through the world, slowing down, shedding our notions and concepts of things, and taking things in as they really are."

And soon after the world-gripping 2019 fire that may well have obliterated Our Lady of Paris, the Notre-Dame Cathedral de Paris, the Rev. Timothy A. R. Cole of Washington DC opined "Beauty and faith are far more closely linked than our current age allows. We listen to music; we stare at a glorious sunrise or at the trees bedecked with blossoms; we sense something beyond us, something sacred. But we cannot grasp what it means. We only know that it is profound and precious and somehow close to the heart of things."

Seeking to make friends with beauty itself, whether it be natural or man-made, is precisely why working with ancient peoples may be part of the spoken medicine that we need to live with the earth.

Since 1926, a modified Lakota language emerged that is more easily translatable into English than the original language because it became more noun-based. But the whole of the old Lakota language is in verbs. For Western minds to be able to perceive value in the original and old indigenous perspectives, it is important to find ways of seeing all of life, including ourselves, as verbs.

As a living meditation, Lakota elder Lawrence Hunter chronicles the symbol of 'spiritual food' in traditional Lakota spirituality:

"Before an Indian takes a drink of water and passes it to his people, he pours some on Mother Earth. It is an offering of thanksgiving for the ones that Mother Earth took to her bosom so that these spirit people can partake of the water. In spiritual food, the four foods offered are water, meat, corn, and fruit because they are the only ones that the Indians had.

One gives a piece of food, not a big one, nor too small, but just so. The right amount goes a long way."

More than a century since the Wounded Knee Massacre in 1890, an event that ended active resistance against the U.S. government, Lakota elders are now sharing their belief that this spirituality is indigenous to every man and woman. No separation. Native spirituality is for everyone—native peoples and Western peoples, Americans and Asians, the sum of all human culture.

*Lakota elders are now sharing their belief that this spirituality is indigenous to every man and woman. No separation. Native spirituality is for everyone—native peoples and Western peoples, Americans and Asians, the sum of all human culture.*

Paul Steinmetz leaves an impression, in *Meditations With The Lakota: Prayers, Songs, and Stories of Healing and Harmony*, that "The distance between the religions, be they traditional Indian, Christian, or Peyote," is very small on the level of personal meditation:

> "Native American Spirituality is part of Technological Man, a part of himself that he has repressed into his unconscious. It is for this reason that Native Americans can help Technological Man get in touch with his own primal

roots. This is the only way he will redeem the world of nature, which he has been exploiting and polluting. No program nor plan will accomplish this. It must be a spirituality that expresses itself with nature. From this personal relationship flow a love and respect toward nature, a willingness not to dominate and an ability to view creation sacramentally. But Technological Man must not only bring up this spirituality from his own primal unconscious, he must also assimilate the contents into his own conscious life, a process Carl Jung called individuation…and…time is running out. There is a sense of urgency. This spirituality is not a luxury but a necessity."

Steinmetz concludes decisively that by inviting all nations to recognize their interdependence with one another and with the Earth, Native Americans can help modern man and woman find "a personal relationship with Nature and a willingness to view creation as sacred."

*If we decide we want to have no more separation between the Earth and we humans, we need to acknowledge that we have no separation from each other.*

If we decide we want to have no more separation between the Earth and we humans, we need to acknowledge that we have no separation from each other. This is the awareness we need within ourselves to make it through. Globally, and wherever it is that you or I call home today, we have plenty to do about sustainability, cleaning up our acts, unlocking communication, and mending fences; but most important are our communal choices—making friends.

Most of us will not rise to summits of yoga mastery, but the precepts where sincerity and surrender are intertwined, are accessible to all. The Mother, Mirra Alfassa, said, "Each one receives it according to his sincerity. It does not depend on outward circumstances but on a sincere aspiration and openness." Wherever you are coming from—rich or poor or temporarily stuck in some kind of purgatory, stuck between our own past and present desire for change—you can achieve sincere aspiration and surrender.

Rather, she guides the seeker to "Let your sincerity and surrender be genuine; when you give yourself, give completely, without demand, without condition, without reservations… nothing to be left to the ego or given to any other power. The more complete your faith, sincerity, and surrender, the more will grace and protection be with you." The path of surrender is safe and sure.

On November 28, 1913, The Mother dated a beautiful prayer that beseeches us to see a better version of ourselves as we raise our vibration with the Earth itself.

# Prayer

*for*
*Making Friends*

# "Bring to the Earth and to Men a Little More of Pure Light and True Peace"

By The Mother (Mirra Alfassa)

*"Grant that this day which is about to
dawn may bring to the Earth and to men
a little more of pure light and true peace;
may Thy manifestation be more complete,
and Thy sweet law more widely recognised;
may something higher, nobler, more true
be revealed to mankind; may a vaster
and deeper love spread abroad so that
all painful wounds may be healed; and
may this first sunbeam dawning upon the
Earth be the herald of joy and harmony, a
symbol of the glorious splendour hidden in
the essence of life."*

# This Thing Called Love

26
Nov.
2018

Dear Ann,
Every time
you smile, it
is a reminder of
the sweetness of
giving freely. The
source of happiness
found within. There are
miracles happening all around.
The Jain attitude says people are
blind with their knowledge:
"Drop your knowledge. Knowledge
is worthless; wonder is precious.
Regain the wonder that you had when you
were a child — and the kingdom of God
belongs only to those who are able to become
children again."        The Bodhi Tree leaf
known as Bo — sacred fig tree,
was born in India    heart-shaped,
is a living presence    of gazing with
gratitude!
        → Richard
        Hanuman                Happiest and
                        earliest to you
                        Always.

Richard J. Marks, *Tree of Awakening Gratitude*, 2018. Written in ink on a fresh Bodhi fig tree leaf at Pushkar Lake, a prominent spot of pilgrimage in the Ajmer district of Rajasthan, as well as the site of the world-famous Pushkar Fair.

This is a very special chapter because I'm arriving somewhere entirely new with you. I never thought I'd be finding out for myself what love is actually supposed to do. As we place our attention on love itself, the desire for freedom begins anew. The footsteps we have taken have progressed toward freedom, so it is time now not to just see, but to do. Lifting up your heart, not just for a moment, but for a lifetime. It all begins in the body.

## *It all begins in the body.*

Venturing deep into Rajasthan, India in 2018, five of us were privileged to have an expedition centered around tiger and wildlife conservation. A trip to Nature in India is a panoramic symbol of the wild, a place to be connected to life unharnessed, not for outings to temples or spiritual yoga, but for being with animals and people.

My list of the wildlife we encountered exceeds fifty spectacular animal species and communities, from the kingdoms of minute dragonflies, to five-stripe squirrels, white-throated kingfishers, demoiselle cranes, woodpeckers, and Indian scopes owls; from stately Royal Bengal tigers, Sambar deer, Niglai antelope, water buffalo, and Ganges soft-shell turtles to carnivorous Bengal monitor lizards capable of reaching lengths as long as three meters (ten feet).

One of the most striking things to be noticed on India's highways is how people and cargo are lavishly decorated. In India, trucks are as richly decorated as people. It's over the top. A common analogy of the trucks describes them as if they are "gigantic women, like second wives," which could explain why the trucks are decorated with paint and 'jewelry.' We decorated our bus, moving across the desert flatlands, and up came the subject of our own ancestors. Our Indian guide, Rajveer Singh, noted that we were traveling along the Aravalli Mountain Range of Rajasthan, the oldest fold mountains of India, running across Rajasthan to Haryana.

We named our Grandmothers, traveling their names across the land ...

*Dana's: Vervain and Ivette*

*Terry's: Gertrude and Alberta*

*Annie's: Dorothy and Ann*

*Richard's: Helen and Myrtle*

*Amy's: Oradell and Catherine*

Grateful to have made it to India's mountaintops, at Pushkar, we climbed the two pilgrims' mountains. People who make the ascent receive the ancestral priestly prayers and many fully bathe in Lake Pushkar amidst priests decadently removed from the world in the yogi temple. All pilgrims are marked with the authentic Indian powder made from turmeric and other local materials used for social and religious markings; when mixed with slaked lime, the rich yellow powder turns red.

"Prayers!" I said aloud at the Ganesha Temple in Ranthambore, "strength, moral strength—reinforced, repaired."

Like a child who demands 'tell me why,' I began to ask what was entering my soul. What can love see that nothing else can? Why is love real?

Like naming our Grandmothers, we have to name what we are seeking. Our problems start when we continue to wait on naming what is in our hearts. That is your call to action.

> *Our problems start when we continue to wait on naming what is in our hearts. That is your call to action.*

### Arriving In The Body.

In Paris, La Pagode is a Japanese pagoda and garden that was built in 1895 for François Emile Morin, the owner of the department store Le Bon Marché. Ever since it opened to the public in the 1930s, it has been the center of avant-garde cinema. When Marc, a French economist, went to see the film *The King's Speech* in 2010 at the historic La Pagode Cinema, he had no expectation about what he was about to see.

As the film started, he was taken by the capacity of the King to free himself. "This guy, Prince Albert, was able to overcome his obstacle: either the constraints that his body, or his mind, created," Marc recalls from that moving storyline. England's Prince Albert must ascend the throne as King George VI, but he has a speech impediment, a stammer that he never fully overcame. An Australian actor and speech therapist teaches the monarch how to speak with confidence.

Marc sees himself in parallel to Prince Albert, who was "looking for freedom, for a way, out of these constraints."

"Show them you're the best" is Marc's indelibly tattooed approach to life. An outright perfectionist, he ostensibly has it all: his family loves him, his career has been illustrious, he is universally well-liked, his ego is in check, and he is generous to a fault. For his generation's values, he's everything a perfect person should and can be.

Yet, by the age of thirteen, he had self-imposed such severe psychological constraints, he frequently couldn't speak when he was waking up in the morning. The perfect boy developed an odd behavior. "I thought I wasn't able to exhale; actually, I was not able to inhale deeply enough." He had to get help to learn how to breathe. "To be able to exhale well," he explains, "you need to inhale well—to breathe out better with the belly. Not with my lungs, but with my belly—the center."

Strangely enough, 'inhale' and 'aspire' are the same in French. The Latin verb 'spirare,' meaning 'breathe,' is indeed the source of a number of verbs. On the authority of wordsmith Mark Nichol, 'aspire' literally means 'breathe on.' The connotation is that one breathes heavily with the exertion of aspiring to a goal. The modern sense of 'aspire' is 'try to be or do something,' and the noun form 'aspirant' refers to someone who is a candidate or contestant.

Marc reflects that the difficulty in his body, unconsciously, was that he didn't aspire deeply enough. "I did not dare to reach my goals." He now sees how he was preventing himself from aspiring to "a different world...a world without the constraints of being the first, the best, the wisest, the calmest, the best...boy."

He continued to pay a price. The price has been extreme limits on his self-expression. He sought to quiet the relationship he began with himself so long ago, buried deep down in his body, down in his legs. Yet it didn't go away; it hid itself. A grown man, he failed at times to be able to walk. Pushed all the way to a wheelchair, his anger compacted far down into the lower body. A far distance from his mind, where it all began and existed.

A therapist helped him understand his inability to walk was psychological and wondered why no one had told him that self-love was not reaching him. Being the best at everything, self-worth was not Marc's problem, but why was the healing aspect of such self-hatred avoided?

Again turning to the Latin, it seems as if he was pressuring himself into perfection ('*perfectus*'), whereas he may have had a far easier road had he, rather, gone to the Greek ('*telios*'), which can mean 'perfect' but is more usually used to refer to maturity or wholeness. Self-love, in the body and mind, would have shown him that there is power in imperfection. Perfection is not what we should be aiming for. Far from it.

There is power in imperfection. Perfection is not what we should be aiming for. Far from it.

When a ceramic or porcelain breaks, especially in museums, the pieces are rejoined with camouflaged adhesive; but alternately, the Japanese have respect for showing what is broken. 'Kintsugi' pottery is the art of repairing broken pottery with a special tree sap dusted with powdered gold, silver, or platinum. Once completed, evokes Paris muse and art historian Kelly Richman-Abdou, "Beautiful seams of gold glint in the conspicuous cracks of ceramic wares," giving a one-of-a-kind appearance to each 'repaired' piece.

In addition to serving as an aesthetic principle, '*Kintsugi*' is related to the Japanese philosophy of '*wabi-sabi*', which calls for seeing beauty in the flawed or imperfect. She helps us see much that gets born in the repair method of allowing flaws to shine through: the Japanese feeling of '*mottainai*,' which expresses regret when something is wasted, as well as '*mushin*,' the acceptance of change. We are called to be who we are, with all our cracks and imperfections.

> *We are called to be who we are,*
> *with all our cracks and imperfections.*

A strong impression arose, as Marc walked out of *The King's Speech*, about the way he saw himself. The first thing that came into his mind was: *I have the right to express myself.* But it's odd, he recalls, because while for himself it was "the right to express," Prince Albert, on the other hand, "had a duty to do it, because while the United Kingdom was involved in the war against Germany, he was the one who would influence the people in the streets."

Marc is now a keynote speaker at many events. He speaks about the power of his own voice, not only in words but also in sounds and music. "When singing," he says, "you express something of who you really are, because of the sound you issue." Yet, to this day, when asked to sing in public, he doesn't dare.

But there's hope: he sees a way to get self-love into the body. And the way in, rather than through words, is sharing music with others. The verb he uses for music is 'to share.' He enjoys listening and being in his body; but equally, he enjoys how music gets him out of his body, and out of his constraints.

"Somebody has written the music; somebody is performing the music; somebody is listening to music; this is sharing for me." How he brings love into and out of the body, just like breathing in and out, is in sharing the experience of music with others. Marc sees singing as healing with others.

Like Marc, I'm shy to sing much in public, except in Marie's Crisis, and I don't whistle when I'm happy. But singing is one of the things I also love to do.

One of the best places, anywhere on earth for that, is in Marie's Crisis, a below-ground bar in New York City. Marie's Crisis bar was built in 1839, named after Marie Du Mont, an Austrian immigrant well known for her blond hair, her voice, and for selling alcohol during Prohibition (1920-1933). This place, where people come from all over the world to sing unlimited show tunes, opened in the 1850s as a prostitutes' den, lasted through

Prohibition, when it was known as Marie's (the 'Crisis' came from the 'Crisis' pamphlets by American Independence hero Thomas Paine, who died in the same house).

I often look around the room, seeing the faces of other people who are completely engaged with their hearts in the pleasure of the song. There's a great delight in watching each individual person but also benefiting from a whole room of people wholly engaged in song together; that's also true when going to a big concert, and into places of worship.

Somebody once turned to me in Marie's Crisis. Over the music, he said, "We need more of this in the world." I knew exactly what he meant because it shouldn't exist only in a tiny downstairs bar for just sixty or seventy people to enjoy. If more people across the world could experience more frequently what we could in Marie's Crisis, we would probably be a lot nicer, a lot friendlier, toward each other. We would see that we're supposed to be singing.

*We would see that we're supposed to be singing.*

*And yes, it is this thing called love.*

And yes, it is this thing called love. We can communicate new ways of seeing through music. It's bringing it into the body: bringing the music and love in, and letting the old fear go, that creates space for joy and integration.

## Receive Love By Giving It.

We name our Grandmothers for this reason: all re-training and re-education requires the wisdom of the past. It can be given to us now if we seek it. We must move forward with that vast and vital faculty of memory. We all want to feel our dream is lived out in someone after us; and it's true, much of our wisdom comes from our forebears, and weighs in directing who we feel should be.

But with a glint of irony, your freedom isn't found in your forebears. It very well may be the other way around, that the freedom of all time—past, present, and future—comes into this world through you. With compassion, I can think about their lives, all my ancestors, male and female, going all the way back to the beginning of time.

*The freedom of all time—past, present and future—comes into this world through you.*

In their own ways, many of my ancestors have been through what I have been through, very likely carrying a Pain-Body and bitter emotions not yet released. My grandmother would have loved more adult education; my mother would have liked a loving father... and so it goes. That ancestral bitterness might still be within you.

Yes, it's in your body, and interestingly, there is actually something good you can do for the ancestors. It's high time to do something for all who came before you and for those who shall come after.

This wisdom is passed down from generation to generation. "A lifetime," wrote the Roman philosopher Seneca to his friend, "is the only property a person has. It must be used fully and to its depths." Here is where your aspiration, sincerity, and determination for freedom returns straight to the center stage.

It is not what we have that matters, but how we hold it, how we frame it in our consciousness, and its meaning to us. To say it another way, for the word of God to come into this world and take root in our flesh, we have to take responsibility. As The Mother says in the book *Love Treasures*, "Calling on God to do everything and save one all the trouble and struggle is a deception and does not lead to freedom and perfection."

*The source of happiness is found within us. And in the living present, that happiness and victory are always to be shared with others.*

The source of happiness is found within us. And in the living present, that happiness and victory is always to be shared with others. But truly beware of rushing back to 'fix' whoever and whatever you left behind in your Big Goodbye or being distracted again, by what may be in front of you. If you must, stop and do another Big Goodbye, or even two; do it. But don't regress or go backward. Press on.

In the mornings when I awaken, if I feel the smallest bit off, I check myself very carefully to see where there may be a disturbance of the mind. If I feel strange, I try to locate where it is in the body. Is it in the heart, the forehead, in my back? I don't rush out of bed on mornings when I feel out of balance; or run to a gym or into a yoga studio to try to twist the stress out of my muscles; I don't distract myself with texting.

I use everything I have learned to quiet myself. Pain and fear, when they arise, must be felt to their full force. Then it is possible and even necessary to transmute that fear into meaning and love. Be on your guard, be ever watchful. Keep the temple of the body clean.

> *Pain and fear, when they arise,*
> *must be felt to their full force.*

This is the best time for prayers, of your own making or choosing, to set your day.

To accomplish the things I want, I ask of myself: *'does it serve me?'* If the answer is no, then it is no matter to be concerned about. We have already learned that to concern ourselves with those things that do not matter, brings us straight back to pain. Move only with an affirmative to what serves you.

The freedom we can attain is not found in loss; it is not found in laws and constitutions; it is not even found in surrender. It's found in you. And there is always a process.

If we've seen anything in our journey, it is that you the reader and I the writer are one thing: the healer.

We hear the call to action, to heal the Earth, but more than a few secular leaders, businesspeople, entrepreneurs, indigenous peoples, and even rabbis, oppose the misconception of 'repair-rhetoric.' We are not doing the right thing by trying to save everything and thereby save ourselves.

Rabbi K. A. Korff, too, challenges the overuse, and misuse, of concepts that over-emphasize it is our job to save everything. The Jewish concept of 'Tikkun Olam' is commonly defined by acts of kindness to 'perfect' or 'repair 'the world.

With this popular credo, Korff complains, "It is so very difficult, indeed utterly unbearable, to sit silently by while Jews, and now the general religious and secular communities, completely misuse and distort the term 'Tikkun Olam'—certainly not intentionally or out of any malice, but rather out of ignorance in the pursuit of virtuous goals and principles, which may be applicable to general society and civilization… we cannot, and are not instructed to save the world, or even to repair it. Judaism teaches no such thing."

Rather, he says, "We are instructed to conduct ourselves properly…and in that way to contribute to society and civilization both by example and through practice and action."

The body holds all that we need: love, music, divinity, self-expression, ancestors. In the present moment, where we're in a place of power, we can learn to 'unpretend.' Flip the moral admonishment around from "don't pretend to be something you're not," turning it into "you don't have to pretend to not be something you are."

In this way, 'the thing called love' resides in our sincerity, and our bodies receive love by giving it. It is a reminder of the sweetness of giving freely.

# Prayer

*for*
*This Thing Called Love*

# "Tree of Awakening Gratitude"

By Richard J. Marks

*Every time you smile, it is a reminder*
*of the sweetness*
*of giving freely.*
*The source of happiness is found within.*
*There are miracles happening all around.*
*The Jain attitude says people are blind with their knowledge:*

*"Drop your knowledge.*
*Knowledge is worthless.*
*Wonder is precious.*
*Regain the wonder that you had*
*When you were a child*
*— and the kingdom of God belongs only to those who are able*
*to become children again."*

*This Bodhi tree leaf, known as Bo — a sacred fig tree —*
*was born in India*
*and heart-shaped,*
*is a living presence of gazing with gratitude.*

---

\*   This prayer is pictured at the opening of this chapter. In India, I
plucked and inscribed a 'bodhi tree' leaf, from a large and very old fig
tree, where the women continually gather and walk clockwise around
the tree with strings, saying and singing prayers. Also called a Bo tree,
according to Buddhist tradition, it is where the Buddha sat when he
attained Enlightenment ('Bodhi').

# Epilogue —
# Freedom
# Travels

One morning in the elevator of my building at Gramercy Park in New York City, a quiet and safe Victorian neighborhood in the midst of Manhattan, I met a woman whose movers were carrying a table into the hallway. "Good move, I hope," I said. She kept her eyes down. "Where to?" I asked.

In her tote bag were bottles of expensive perfumes. She said, looking directly at me, "I actually don't know."

I said as softly as possible: "People will be generous…and help you along the way."

"Thanks," she said, "I appreciate that."

In the subway, I carried an elderly man's walker up the flights of stairs. "Can't think of anything better," he said, without looking up but smiling.

As my eyes match the movement of my feet, I see what is in front of me. And that way of seeing reveals that, as American spiritual teacher Ram Dass has said, "When you know how to listen, everybody is the guru."

*Observe how you travel outwardly because that is how you travel inwardly.*

*They are the same.*

Observe how you travel outwardly because that is how you travel inwardly. They are the same. If I am looking for escape outwardly, I'll feel I have it once I'm finally resting in someone's arms, despite that it passes as soon as I wake up and no one is there. When the intention is to unearth something beautiful, I do not seek rest, but to travel fearlessly. This is important, for I'm not leaving my soul to rest when I travel. I'm going out to find it. That means all the time. It means now, and then now, and then now again.

My feelings change along the way; that is maturity. For in travel, seeking clues to my own human nature takes discipline and facing difficulty, action and obligation.

Every time I give love and attention to where I am, I find the truth of my prayers. For in every locale where I have traveled, I gained more than I bargained for; more than self-diagnostic 'results' such as healing, reconciliation or quieting. I didn't seek or plan for these.

Travel happens in steps, progressively, but in freedom, something else happens. It is seeing the whole picture. Having journeyed through this book toward new freedom, how would you now approach not only your own problems differently but also another person's? How do you see, and hence, apply the seven footsteps to someone other than yourself? How do you approach another person who is in some way constricted, and show them another way ahead?

*Travel happens in steps, progressively, but in freedom, something else happens. It is seeing the whole picture.*

In 'Freedom to Share,' we covered ground about why we feel stuck, with Rev. Suarez recommending that we rid ourselves of the stuff that doesn't work for us anymore. As individuals, as well as citizens of the world, in communities, in our governments, the journey to freedom is about the whole lot of us. And now, we have to actually do it.

A collective action, perhaps, is to make this a story of rebirth. In the Western tradition, rebirth is a way of traveling; not to selfishly gather things and embellish our curiosity, but to embody hope for nonviolent change.

Elementary school students who learn to write stories have made a list of examples of rebirth stories that redeem, among them *Beauty and the Beast, It's A Wonderful Life, E.T.: The Extra-Terrestrial, Snow White, The Handmaid's Tale,* and *The Lion King.* In the West, rebirth stories have three main components. First, identify the traumatic experience and awaken to a new beginning. From this, low self-worth increases following the discovery of one's potential. Inner conflict subsides as the kinder side of one's character wins over the selfish self.

The true purpose of the 2015 film *Mad Max: Fury Road,* writes Miranda Auer of Colorado State University, is to portray the rebirth of a world that seems to be beyond hope. The answer to "Who or what can bring about the rebirth of the world?" is given in the film's conclusion, leaving the viewer to ponder what implications this has in our own world. In answer to the second question, "Who saves the world?" the film's approach gives the clue for what we face now.

"The people who hope, and keep hoping, and are willing to fight and die for that hope, but who do not kill needlessly for it," Auer answers. "The ones who want to live in peace, not die in glory. In short, in the world of *Mad Max: Fury Road*—the women. This is why the story centers around their journey—Max is just along for the ride."

In literature, Charles Dickens' novel, *A Christmas Carol*, is an example of the rebirth process: Scrooge acts selfishly and overworks his clerk Bob Cratchit. A great tale of an inner change that comes from a strange journey within, *A Christmas Carol* depicts the overnight visit of three ghosts who help Scrooge understand what he had done wrong with his life. After his journey, he changes his ways, gives Cratchit a raise, befriends Tiny Tim, and acts with generosity and love.

*This is freedom: seeing how to transition from a life with dwindling hope to a world in which freedom connects with both empathy and power. When they connect, we have hope.*

In non-Western traditions, such as Buddhism, there are also things we have to get rid of, but with non-attachment rather than rebirth.

Tim McHenry, the Chief Programmatic Officer at the Rubin Museum of Art in New York City, was astonished by the story of a Tibetan Lama, a regular Buddhist practitioner who, in the 1950s, was incarcerated and tortured by the Chinese. After decades, when she was liberated and was able to come to India and ultimately to the West, she would say the only way she could get through that experience was by exercising compassion and forgiveness for her captors and torturers, by acknowledging they did not have the freedom that she has to love. "That's pivoting toward that enlightenment," explains McHenry, "where the first thing that you've actually got to get rid of, which will ever-constrain you, is hatred." This is freedom: seeing how to transition, from a life with dwindling hope, to a world in which freedom connects with both empathy and power. When they connect, we have hope.

Where freedom resides for normal human behavior, McHenry says, is in the limitations that are placed on us (as in the moving story above), or the limitations we place on ourselves (such as those Scrooge places on himself). McHenry, who spends valuable time with teachers of non-Western wisdom traditions—a diverse range of perspectives from community organizers, contemporary artists and spiritual leaders—observes that freedom comes about as an experience when you limit your options. Boundaries, a form of discipline, are needed to have a genuine sense of freedom.

Counter-intuitive to that, he says, "Abnormal human behavior is enlightenment. *That is total freedom, and that is what we call liberation.* You actually free yourself from constraints because you're not attached to anything. That's a whole different ball of wax. But in conventional behavioral terms, we need the constraints."

Our collective karma, he says sadly, is climate change. "We can't cope well with untrammeled freedom and liberty. And that's why we need constraints…it's why communities exist; because if you were just left to your own devices, you probably wouldn't have the time to have the freedom to express who you are."

Traveling the journey of freedom, how will you choose to approach the problems you want to fix? Instead of thinking about how you would try to fix them or allowing yourself to struggle alone—remember the power of your sincerity, self-worth, and prayers. These help foster a loving world where people make friends.

Remember the power of your sincerity, self-worth, and prayers. But be forewarned against the transgression of taking what you should not have. Certainly, not everything that I did was actually meant for me.

I would like to now reveal the other half of Norma Tringaldi's maxim "Life is a mystery to be lived, not a problem to be solved." The other half of that maxim is like having the other half of a heart locket: "Get off the Cross, somebody needs the wood." There are mysteries out there to be loved and sanctified, to be expressed in your deepest prayers and feelings.

She was saying, when you get out of hell and throw all that disappointment into the fire, you prove something else. You are proving you are worthy of love, and you are willing to live. Travel is how we gain such experience. The nature of human restlessness creates trans-cultural rapport.

Through outward travel, I have found people who are a clear lens that enables me to wonder. Because I am a traveler, I learn for myself through direct contact. This explains why I don't have a lot of patience for tour guides who rush me through sacred sites and into the shopping plazas. They don't like me much, either, when I tell them to go on ahead without me. Therefore, it is not what I see when I travel but how I allow it to be experienced intact, that has become more important than ever.

In all kinds of communion, what matters is not where you go, but how. The motif to always err on the side of generosity is expansive.

We can heal ourselves and others simply by being together, by listening, by living close to what we perceive to be sacred, whether it is the love of someone, music, or ceremony, a reconciliation or mediation between warring conflicts.

Even with all the Big Goodbyes I've had to say, I'm still a cautious person. When it gets scary and unexpected, when the path you never chose has chosen you, it is natural to distrust and fear. In the traveling phase of life, we may go far, feeling at times that we have tasted sacred knowledge, and yet not be fed by it.

That, too, has changed in my outlook. The key is to not take what is not yours.

In the cold light of the present, it is a form of colonial thinking to transgress the sacred rites, ceremony, knowledge, and philosophy encountered in travel. The beautiful poetry and ceremonial songs of civilization may be stored in the inaccessible vaults of the British Museum but digging around in there will never uncover the essential mystery of the human heart. The human heart is not a museum in which we can hide our own truth from others. Knowledge does not enjoy a copyright, even if it is guarded.

*The human heart is not a museum in which we can hide our own truth from others. Knowledge does not enjoy a copyright, even if it is guarded.*

When we travel, what brings together the spiritual and the physical is when we are invited to witness each other's sacred prayers. Some mysteries are very old but very much alive. Inside song and poetry are intact original languages that can be traced back as far as 30,000 years.

For twenty-five years, I have taken it upon myself to directly encounter old societies that have survived imperialism and empire, the really old places that still exist, before they become enveloped in globalization. Year by year, fewer very ancient cultures and languages prevail. Computer and business parks, modern industrial development, and technologies are imposed.

When traveling to what is most remote and far-reaching, in almost every pilgrimage, someone or something will invite you into sacred knowledge. On the journey of the self to the self, just as you did not come with that knowledge, you don't leave with it. What you gain is the ability to make transitions, moment to moment, to walk with new eyes in both the spiritual and the physical. We focus too much on the conflict between the two. Enter the body and register yourself as a participant, so you can see the details, the transitions, the love in giving and sharing yourself.

Love is something you build, and which builds you. Just as Notre Dame de Paris still stands after the great fire, so too will our common home and our common destiny.

Do partake in what is yours to take, but again, do not go against that wise admonition from Edie Dushkin Soeiro to not make someone else's mistakes. Make your own mistakes.

What is it you want now—a hero's finale? What if I were to tell you that seeing beauty is where the courage comes from to change? It is in finding beauty that the strength comes to conquer anything.

*Seeing beauty is where the courage comes from to change. It is in finding beauty that the strength comes to conquer anything.*

In the seven footsteps, you took a divorce from corrupted freedom. Your peace and quiet shut out the false personality of your fears. You shed old skins and put on new ones.

In beauty is awareness.

# Prayer

*for*
*Epilogue — Freedom Travels*

# "Creed for Awakening"

By Richard J. Marks

*I forgive human pride.*
*I forgive the totality of human hatred.*

*Turn away from the ocean and look at the beach.*
*What am I to look at?*
*What's on the beach? Who's there?*

*The first thing I see is beauty.*

*In creation, I see colors,*
*myriad life in graceful perfection.*
*One sees all colors and flight of wings.*
*People have not yet existed.*
*We are not in a post-human world,*
*but a world without the human.*
*Humanity has not yet been born.*

*What do I see myself doing here?*

*First, as interesting as it is to be an observer,*
*one has to be quiet*
*to realize*
*one is being observed, too.*

*Love is the witness.*

*It's like that. If one imagines that there is no obstacle, there
is no longer any experience except of the light.
It's more than an island.
It's freedom from identity.*

*What am I doing here?*

*I see a beach and a coastline,
the colors are more vivid,
a world without a concept of pollution. Industrialization is
conceptually unthinkable.*

*It is so simple and clear.
I am here to love.*

*I open my eyes.*

*I am in recovery of my heart, soul and dream.
I bring love into the world.
I stand up for myself and speak my truth.
I take care of myself and nurture my spirit.
I let go of what could go wrong.*

*I reflect now on allies*
*and envision their active presence,*
*in my actions,*
*relationships,*
*employment.*

*I am not a consumption-centric human.*

*We seek love.*
*We seek freedom.*
*We seek abundant life.*

*Be on time. Be prepared.*

*May your love always be.*
*And so Rise.*
*To the Sun.*

Odilon Redon (1840-1916). *Le Bouddha*
(The Buddha), 1907. Musée d'Orsay, Paris.

# About the Book

---

*RISE TO THE SUN* is a progression of footsteps that symbolize the way forward and help in navigating our way through rough waters, whether personal, collective, or spiritual in nature. Making it safely across—to the other side of fear, grief, and trauma, travailing all the bumps and pains—is not something we easily see or feel at the outset.

The goal of this book is to renew and transform ourselves in order to be more joyful, resilient, and creative in taking on what we care about most. After all those Big Goodbyes, it should come as a relief we are living in the era ready for a Big Hello. Hello to harmony between humanity, nature, and the environment. Hello to sincere aspiration in the face of adversity and challenge.

Hello to new friends because nothing else speaks of safety and security quite the way making friends does. Therefore, when entering a path of finding new awareness, let go of defensiveness. Let go of pride. We can't be of service or make friends that way.

"Put the spiritual first, not second, and see what happens." I took Shelby Perkins' words to heart just before my first trip to India. Free at last from the constraints of her training as an environmental attorney, Perkins is now an artist, a farmer, a thinker, and grower of grapes. For more than a decade, she and I have been on unique and parallel life journeys to finding freedom. She, and many like her whom I have come to struggle alongside, know, love and cherish...we come through the worst because of each other, we heal together, and we uproot our despair together. Transforming ourselves is very beautiful, and we are just beginning.

Expand your sense of adventure. It will inspire you to keep going with the steep climb.


## Why Bother?

Climate grief is now a thing. Support groups exist for it, with phrases appearing on 'how to cope' and headlines stating, "I have felt hopelessness over climate change." If you're suffering from climate grief, you're not alone. Under this intense pressure, the notion that we must fix what is wrong has turned to collective grief.

The causes of climate crisis have determinately pressed on so long and far that professors and climate scientists, like Dr. Steve Running at the University of Montana, have identified and developed "Five Stages of Climate Grief" equivalent to the death of a loved one: denial, anger, bargaining, depression, and acceptance. Now that all nations have reached that fifth phase—acceptance—we are in need of self-transformation, rather than going out to fix what can't be fixed.

The purpose of all activism is to bring about change in society. Activism is a form of freedom of expression and free thought. From startups and meet-ups, to purging injustice and changing whole societies, it is an attempt to reform the world. In history, activism has led people to new freedoms. When we take up freedom as our life-long aspiration, it lights our way out of hell.

No need to go on making ourselves feel we can't be free or succumbing to people who may judge or persecute us for wanting to change. As hard as it may seem, as self-evident as this sounds, let's move forward without them.

Let's set that goal firmly in our hearts.

## Why Forgive?

There is a pathway letting go of defensiveness in relationships by considering others' points of view. Where there are strong emotions about a situation, people may feel upset or misunderstood. We don't need to agree with these other individuals; we are all simply asked to understand different motivations and have compassion for each other's feelings. This process can positively shift the energy of power struggles, much like letting go of a rope during a tug-of-war. As you see others' points of view, the door opens for creative solutions to enter.

Once we forgive, we can make friends. We need to find all the ways we can to make friends.

## Active Ways to Engage

Remember that people of different orientations and backgrounds use language differently.

Highlight words that appeal to you now.

Activate them by first learning they have multiple meanings.

Don't fight over words of the past.

Pick and use the words you speak from today forward.

Start using that new language in your life.

Trust yourself to find those meanings for yourself.

Your awareness will help others begin, too.

# The 3-Step Recipe (To Keep Your Eyes Open!)

Whenever you need to pause—to see and perceive before you react—remember this blueprint that has already been shown to you in the stories within this book.

## I. Break free

*Meaning:* 'Breaking Free from Hell' boils down to rejecting freedom that has been corrupted.

Endurance, forgiveness, and resilience are sometimes not enough: we must release our mounting grief and end our suicide. We have much collective trauma, but we have hope. We are in an age of healing ourselves and our planet. That means we are each called to task to release all that blocks love from flowing through us.

*Action:*

Find freedom by taking personal responsibility for your relationships and by loving yourself.

## II. Retrain yourself

*Meaning:* Expand your awareness and diminish reactivity.

Our own feelings are the cause of our problems, and not the world or the people in it. It is our own feelings that we struggle so hard and long against. And above all, due to our own thinking, we are responsible for everything that happens to us.

Education and strenuous love are at the core of change. In science, nothing is discovered without straying. In art, being lost is the precondition of creation. In apprenticeship, nothing can be learned without the experience of failure. To *enjoy* being lost also presumes the special quality of curiosity. Curiosity is what enables us to learn from losing our way, to make discoveries in the unknown. It means being interested in others, never starting off by imposing our own way, being alert for all kinds of differences, and putting one's self in a stranger's place in order to understand your own uniqueness. Curiosity is the most vital quality, and it is indispensable for voyagers of the future. *By getting lost in ourselves we may someday gain self-acceptance. It is a Big Hello: welcome back to the winning team.*

**Action:**

Become a conscious citizen by being genuine in your everyday thoughts and actions.

## III. Find freedom

*Meaning:* Freedom is defined in many ways, but liberation is always found within.

Active prayers, those beautiful phrases of human emotion and truth, help us see hope and beauty and to do for ourselves.

**Action:**

Freedom can heal, be shared, and traveled.

# Bibliography

---

## Dedication

Bates, William. *The Bates Method for Better Eyesight Without Glasses*. New York: Henry Holt and Company, 1940.

Huxley, Aldous. *The Art of Seeing*. New York: Harper & Brothers Publishers, 1942.

*Incandescence at Sunset*, La Teste-de-Busch, 2015. Photograph: Richard J. Marks.

## Prologue

"Frequency of Prayer." Washington DC: Pew Research Center, 2014.

Ida Ten Eyck O'Keeffe (1889-1961). *Variation on a Lighthouse Theme IV*, 1931-32. Oil on canvas. Image courtesy Dallas Museum of Art, photo: Brad Flowers.

## Flushing The Psychic Toilet

*Brave Cadet*, Ridgewood Military Academy, 1978. Image courtesy of Richard J. Marks.

Farber, Madeline. "Kate Spade's husband pens touching tribute to late designer on first anniversary of her death." Fox News, June 8, 2018.

*Farewell to The Family. People Weekly*, March 27, 1978. Photograph: Tandem Productions.

*Les Trois Tetons (*The Three Breasts), 2014. Photograph: Richard J. Marks.

*Mae West*, 1973. Photograph: Allan Warren.

*Moscone, Milk Shot to Death, San Francisco Examiner*, Nov. 27, 1978. Photograph: Gregory Varnum.

*Parade Formation*, Ridgewood Military Academy *Tabard*, Woodland Hills, California, 1966. Image courtesy of Bill Hillendahl.

*VIET NAM VETS*, Library of Congress photograph collection: *U.S. News & World Report* magazine, April 21, 2971. Photograph: Warren K. Leffler.

## Prayers

Andrei Rublev (1360s-1420s). *The Trinity*, 15th century. Tempera on wood. Tretyakov Gallery, Moscow.

Henry, William. "The Awakened Soul: The Lost Art and Science of Ascension and the Ultimate Yoga Experience." Nashville, Tennessee: Blog of William Henry, June 6, 2016.

Norman Rockwell (1894-1978). *Freedom of Worship*, 1943. Illustration for *The Saturday Evening Post*, February 27, 1943.Norman Rockwell Museum Collection, Norman Rockwell Art Collection Trust, NRACT.1973.023. Artwork courtesy of the Norman Rockwell Family Agency.

Sulzberger, C.L. *Go Gentle Into the Night*. Englewood Cliffs, New Jersey: Prentice-Hall, Inc, 1976.

*The Art of Prayer: An Orthodox Anthology*. Compiled by Igumen Chariton, trans. E. Kadloubovsky & E. Palmer. London: Faber & Faber, 1966, p. 16.

## Breaking Free

Churchill, Winston. "Never Give In, Never, Never, Never." Harrow on the Hill, London, United Kingdom: speech delivered at Harrow School, October 29, 1941.

"Paul McCartney premieres new "Who Cares" video with Emma Stone; launches anti-bullying campaign." ABC Radio, 2018.

Zhang Xiaogang. *Mother and Son No. 1*, 2006. Oil on canvas. 160 cm × 200 cm (63" × 78-3/4"). Provided by Zhang Xiaogang, courtesy Pace Gallery.

Zitun, Yoav. "Gaza's abandoned children: Palestinians leaving their babies at border." Tel Aviv, Israel: Ynetnews - Yedioth Media Group, 2015.

## Don't Believe The Pain

*Dance of the Crystals*, Sparkling Hill Resort, Vernon, British Columbia, Canada, 2015. Photograph: Richard J. Marks.

"The Sixth Report of the Okanagan Historical Society 1935." British Columbia Geographical Names Information System: Okanagan Historical Society, 1936.

Tolle, Eckhart. *A New Earth: Awakening to Your Life's Purpose*. New York: Penguin, 2005, p. 162.

Wilson, Bill. *Alcoholics Anonymous*. New York: Works Publishing Company, 1941.

## The Big Goodbye

Bo Bartlett. *The Parabolist*, 1999. Oil on canvas. Gift from Vicki and Kent Logan to the Collection of the Denver Art Museum, 2001.689. © Bo Bartlett. Photography courtesy Denver Art Museum.

Hesse, Hermann. *The Glass Bead Game (Magister Ludi)*. New York City: Holt Rhinehart and Winston, 1969.

Steinmetz, Paul. *Meditations with the Lakota: Prayers, Songs, and Stories of Healing and Harmony*. Rochester, VT.: Bear & Company, 2001, p. 18.

von Franz, Marie Louise. *Projection and Re-Collection in Jungian Psychology: Reflections of the Soul*. La Salle, IL.: Open Court Publishing Co., a division of Carus Publishing Company, 1980, p. 83.

## Personal Responsibility - Relationships

Antoine Watteau (1684-1721). *L'Embarquement pour Cythère* (Embarkation for Cythera), 1717. Oil on canvas. Musée du Louvre, Paris.

Pomarède, Vincent. "Pilgrimage to Cythera." Paris: Musée du Louvre, 2009.

Stevens, José. "Article 5 In The Election Series." Santa Fe, New Mexico: The Power Path, 2017 (online).

## Worthy Of Love

"A Timeline of HIV and AIDS." Washington DC: HIV.GOV (est. 2005) operated by the U.S. Department of Health and Human Services (HHS).

Crawford, Neta C., Professor and Chair of Political Science, Boston University; Project Director, The Costs of War project. "Iraqi Citizens." Providence, Rhode Island: The Watson Institute for International and Public Affairs, Brown University, 2018.

*Message to Congress — The State of the Union*, January 6, 1941. Courtesy of the Franklin D. Roosevelt Presidential Library.

Nichols, Chris. "Mike Pence's Support for Conversion Therapy Not a Settled Matter." San Francisco: The California Report, KQED News, July 28, 2016.

Proctor, Charlie. "The Queen's Cousin Becomes First Member of The Royal Family to Reveal He is Gay." London: Royal Central, September 18, 2016.

## Freedom To Share

*Kaianerekowa Hotinonsionne: The Great Law of Peace of the Longhouse People*. Translation by Ka-Hon Hes, Akwesasne Notes, Ray Tehanetorens. Drawings by John Kahionhes Fadden. Berkeley, CA: Oyate, 1999.

Lawren Harris (1885-1970). *Lake Superior*, 1923. Oil on canvas. The Thomson Collection at the Art Gallery of Ontario, Toronto.

Mills, Joy. "O Hidden Life", *The Theosophist*, Volume 97, June 1976.

## Making Friends

"Empathy? In Denmark They're Learning It In School." Milan, Italy: Morning Future (online), April 26, 2019.

*Georgia O'Keeffe: Exhibition of Oils and Pastels, January 22-March 17, 1939*. New York City: An American Place, 1939. Exhibition catalogue.

Popova, Maria, "Georgia O'Keeffe on the Art of Seeing." Brain Pickings (blog), 2018.

Winslow Homer (1836-1910). *Nuit d'été* (Summer Night), 1890. Oil on canvas. Musée d'Orsay, Paris.

## This Thing Called Love

Eck, Diana L. *India: A Sacred Geography.* New York: Harmony Books, an imprint of the Crown Publishing Group, a division of Random House, Inc., 2012.

Korff, Y. A. "The fallacy, delusion and myth of Tikkun Olam." Jewish News Syndicate (JNS), June 3, 2013.

*Tree of Awakening Gratitude*, 2018. Photograph: Richard J. Marks.

## Epilogue: Freedom Travels

Auer, Miranda. "Who Killed the World? How Can It Be Reborn? The Image of Rebirth in Mad Max: Fury Road." Thomas G. Endres, ed. *The Image of Rebirth in Literature, Media and Society: Proceedings of the 2017 Conference of The Society for the Academic Study of Social Imagery.* Greely, Colorado: The Society for the Academic Study of Social Imagery (SASSI), University of Northern Colorado, July 2017, pp. 1-3.

*Welcoming Descent of Amida Buddha* (Raigō), c. 1270-1333. Japan, Kamakura Period (1185-1333). Hanging scroll; ink, color, gold and cut gold on silk. Mr. and Mrs. William H. Marlatt Fund 1993.42. Photography courtesy of The Cleveland Museum of Art.

## About the Book

Redon, Odilon (1840-1916). *Le Bouddha* (The Buddha), 1907. Oil on canvas. Musée d'Orsay, Paris.

Running, Steve. "5 Stages of Climate Grief." Milltown, Montana: Friends of 2 Rivers (online), 2007.

CPSIA information can be obtained
at www.ICGtesting.com
Printed in the USA
FSHW020702130520
69940FS